CEMETERI
OF ILLINOI

Erected
to the Memory
of Mrs. Nancy. Con
sort of Lewis G.
Collins. Who

CEMETERIES OF ILLINOIS

A Field Guide to Markers, Monuments, and Motifs

HAL HASSEN & DAWN COBB

Manufactured in the United States of America
P 5 4 3 2 1
∞ This book is printed on acid-free paper.

Library of Congress Control Number: 2017936740
ISBN 978-0-252-08265-8 (paperback) | ISBN 978-0-252-09966-3 (e-book)

We dedicate this book to our families.

For Doris, Chris, Ali, and Scarlet
HH

For my son, Matthew
DC

There was a wooden tombstone in the
churchyard that used to tell all about him,
but that's rotten and gone too.

—WASHINGTON IRVING, "Rip van Winkle"

CONTENTS

PREFACE

Burial grounds present us with a strong emotional pull. On the one hand, they are places full of feelings of sorrow and loss. On the other hand, they provide unique opportunities for learning about our past. Upon the death of a loved one, we return to certain places to perform rituals of burial and memorial. Over time, the details and the rituals change. Consequently, what we see in burial grounds informs us about how society alters its view of death and memorialization.

When you visit a burial ground, you may see one grave marker or thousands. The age of the burial ground and length of time it was or has been used affect what you see. We wrote this guide to provide you with the information you need to understand how burial grounds in Illinois have changed and what caused those changes. The more you know about burial grounds, the more interesting they become.

For decades we have been visiting and studying burial grounds because they are wonderful places to learn about history, geology, art, and society. In addition to being tranquil places of solitude and reflection, they also provide a connection to all those buried there and the folks they left behind.

Hal Hassen
Dawn Cobb

ACKNOWLEDGMENTS

The authors would like to acknowledge the many people who have attended our lectures over the years. Their interest, questions, and, most of all, passion for understanding and preserving burial grounds in Illinois inspired us to write this book. For our family and friends, who listened to us speak about what we had seen while traveling throughout Illinois, your patience and suggestions helped us formulate many questions and articulate what we had learned.

Several people read all or portions of this book. The comments of Ian Brown and an anonymous reviewer provided much-needed guidance, and we are grateful for their suggestions and support. Others read only portions, but their comments also proved valuable. These include Marla Gursh, Chris Hassen, and especially Ted Morrissey.

Doris Hassen far surpassed any expectations of support or assistance one might expect from a spouse. The patience and care she exhibited while editing the text was of immeasurable help. Writing and writing well are not the same thing. Her editorial guidance helped make thoughts into sentences. Many thanks.

The Illinois Department of Natural Resources (IDNR) kindly enabled us to use many of the photographs Hal Hassen took while under their employ. The support of various IDNR supervisors during the preparation of this book is greatly appreciated. Will Hinsman created the maps in chapter 7 and appendix A. Angella Morehouse participated in the early development of this book, and the authors are grateful for her support and passion for Illinois burial grounds. The Illinois State Museum provided an archival copy of the

Ogden-Fettie Mound photograph. Peggy B. Perazzo graciously provided permission to use the Montgomery Wards catalog image.

The former and current staff at the University of Illinois Press, especially Lisa Bayer, who first approached us about doing a book, Michael Roux, who was patient and helpful as we traveled a journey neither of the authors had ever traveled before, Jennifer Comeau, whose editorial skills fine-tuned the flow of our book, and Dustin Hubbart, for his assistance with the images. This has been a very rewarding experience, and we are grateful for all the help.

IN MEMORY OF
Thomas Heslep
Who departed this
life Novr 23rd 1835
Aged 62 years & 9
months.

CHAPTER 1
INTRODUCTION

When visiting burial grounds, you will notice they are not all alike. This might cause you to ask questions:

- Why are some markers plain and others more elaborate?
- Why are some markers short while others quite tall?
- Why are some burial grounds disorganized while others are very orderly?
- Why are some burial grounds small and located in the woods while others are very large and located on the edge of cities?
- What is the difference between a burial ground and a cemetery?

This guide addresses these and other questions.

What draws us into burial grounds affects what we see. Burial grounds offer much to see, but if we do not know what to look for, our vision may be limited. If we know how to look, on the other hand, we will understand more. There are grave markers, family plots, fences, roads, and a variety of plants. Different raw materials and marker styles reflect different periods of time. In some burial grounds there seem to be as many different types and styles of grave markers as there are graves. In contrast, the same types and styles of markers can be seen over and over again in other burial grounds. This guide helps you understand why burial grounds look the way they do.

In Illinois, thousands of historical burial grounds from the 1800s and 1900s are scattered across the landscape. They may contain only a single headstone or more than a hundred thousand headstones. Fortunately, these locations can be identified by grave markers that memorialize a loved one or acknowledge a stranger (1.1). While most active burial grounds in Illinois consist of many acres and tens of thousands of burials, it was not always that way. Before

Fig. 1.1. Tomb of an unknown soldier

Fig. 1.2. Large cemetery

there were large commercial cemeteries (1.2), there were small family plots (1.3) and church graveyards (1.4). As the state developed and grew, the places where Illinoisans buried their dead changed. In addition, the way Illinoisans marked graves and memorialized their dead also changed over time.

Traveling across Illinois, you can readily see that both burial grounds and grave markers vary. These differences exist in part because Illinoisans have themselves changed in many ways. Over time, the economy shifted from an agricultural base to an industrial base. Family incomes grew. People moved from farms to urban centers. Travel changed from a reliance on horses to

Fig. 1.3. Family burial ground

Fig. 1.4. Churchyard burial ground

railroads and eventually cars. These changes affected where we buried the dead and how they were memorialized. Marble replaced sandstone as the primary stone used in grave markers and in turn was later replaced by granite. Small family burial grounds were eventually replaced by large commercial cemeteries. The shift in terminology from *burial ground* to *cemetery* is itself a reflection of profound changes in how we came to memorialize the dead (see chapter 4). Changes in burial grounds and grave markings reflect broad social, economic, and technological changes. In some instances, the differences seen in burial grounds also reflect ethnic diversity (1.5).

Some markers are inscribed with only names and dates (1.6), while others contain folk art or expressions of sentimentality and profound loss (1.7, 1.8). Many burial grounds lack spatial organization, while others are carefully designed and look like parks (1.9, 1.10). Burial grounds may be small and located deep in the woods (1.11), or they might contain thousands of graves located in the open and on the edge of large cities (1.12). This guide informs you about how Illinois burial grounds have changed over time and explains the differences you see. We hope you will take the guide with you when visiting a burial ground just as you might take a guide about birds, trees, or mushrooms when exploring nature.

How to Use the Guide

When visiting historical sites, parks, or museums, you can learn information in a variety of ways. There may be brochures, interpretive panels, audio tours, or staff to guide you. In contrast, other than a sign with the name of the burial ground or a person's name on the grave marker itself, burial grounds in Illinois usually do not provide you with any additional information about what you see. This guide provides general and specific information to help you understand what you see. The goals of the book are simple: to describe and explain what you can expect to see, and to identify specific burial grounds for you to visit.

We examine the changes that have occurred over time and explain the reasons for those changes, with sections on grave markers, burial grounds, and the use of iconographic images. For example, the section on grave markers enables you to identify the most common shapes, sizes, and raw materials used. It also explains why markers vary both within and among burial grounds. Several books and websites explore the meaning of the numerous iconographic images depicted in burial grounds; consequently, we do not provide an in-depth discussion on images but focus instead on how the use of these images has changed over time.

We hope that readers will gain a fuller appreciation for how the material culture found in burial grounds enlightens us about social and cultural changes. We also hope that a better understanding of Illinois burial grounds will motivate readers to help preserve these important resources.

Our emphasis is on the period of time beginning in the early 1800s and extending into the mid-1900s, ending with the introduction of granite grave markers and the development of large for-profit cemeteries. Much of the information is based on our observations of the burial grounds throughout Illinois and other states. Photographs (taken in Illinois unless otherwise noted) illustrate common sights.

Fig. 1.5. Russian Orthodox Cemetery

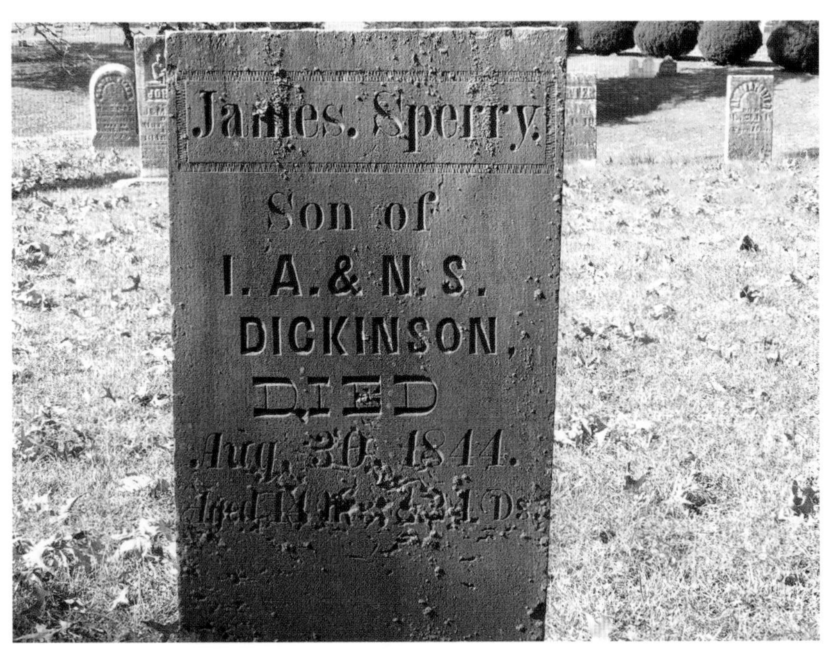

Fig. 1.6. Simple inscription

Fig. 1.7. Folk art

Fig. 1.8. Expression of sorrow

Fig. 1.9. Organization suggesting family plots

Fig. 1.10. Parklike design

Fig. 1.11. Burial ground located in a woods

Fig. 1.12. Community burial ground

In the chapters that follow we examine a variety of topics. Chapter 2 discusses how prehistoric American Indians buried their dead. Although their methods differed from those used by later Illinoisans, their practices, too, changed over time in terms of where the dead were buried and how they were memorialized. Through their shared experience of having to make choices on matters of death and burial, both groups exhibit their common humanity.

Chapter 3 examines the varying ways graves are marked in historical Illinois burial grounds. To a large extent, these differences reflect choices that were influenced by technology, social conditions, economics, and the availability of natural resources. The placement of a particular marker, its general shape, and what may be inscribed on the surface all tell us a lot about both the deceased and those left behind.

Chapter 4 discusses nine different types of burial grounds found in Illinois. Since the early 1800s, Illinois burial grounds have undergone dramatic changes. The small pioneer burial grounds of the earliest settlers have evolved into the large, expansive memorial parks first introduced in the mid-1900s.

Chapter 5 examines the use of iconographic images in burial grounds. These images were used as secular folk art or as religious expressions of profound loss or eternal hope. We examine the type of images used, their general meaning, and why changes have occurred since the early 1800s.

Chapter 6 will help you plan your trips to burial grounds so you can get the most enjoyment and satisfaction from your venture. You will learn how to research and find new burial grounds, what equipment to take, the best way to get acquainted with a site, and proper burial ground etiquette.

Chapter 7 identifies specific public-access burial grounds around Illinois for you to visit. The list provides a wide variety of burial grounds to see. Going to all of the recommended burial grounds does not mean you will see all the sandstone markers from the early 1800s or all the fine "rural cemeteries" in Illinois. Nevertheless, the guide will provide you with the knowledge necessary for setting out on your own. We hope you will be motivated to find additional, unlisted burial grounds, thus experiencing the excitement of discovery for yourself. Keep in mind, however, that many burial grounds are located on private land, and make sure you do not trespass.

Understanding the Past

We are surrounded by visual reminders of the past. Houses (1.13), barns (1.14), commercial buildings, and roads are just a few examples. These structures inform us about broad patterns in the history of Illinois. Professional historians and archaeologists have an easier time interpreting the hidden meanings associated with these older structures than you will, focusing on broad patterns pertaining to architecture and social conditions.

Fig. 1.13. Visible reminder of history

Fig. 1.14. Historical barn

In contrast, burial grounds provide a unique opportunity for ordinary individuals to do what professional historians and archaeologists do: interpret human behavior through the study of material culture. Burial grounds contain a wealth of information. With a basic understanding of the factors affecting the different types of burial grounds and grave markers, you can better interpret what is represented in specific burial grounds. One of the joys of visiting burial grounds is that they inform us about individuals otherwise lost to history, not just about broad patterns. The placement of a particular type and style of grave marker informs us about the deceased, as well as about their friends, neighbors, and families, in ways different from what we learn in history books.

The separation of the dead from the living and the use of grave markers to memorialize the dead are unique human gestures, and people have been burying their dead for tens of thousands of years. Today, most societies bury their dead, but they do it in different ways. A trait shared by most societies is the marking of the grave, primarily with stone, to memorialize the deceased. This action identifies the burial ground as a place where the living and the dead continue to interact. These interactions may be both deeply personal, as when we visit the grave of someone known to us, or more distant, as when we visit a place where strangers are buried. In the latter instance, our appreciation of folk art or history may have drawn us to the site.

Almost all communities have burial grounds. Travel fifteen minutes in any direction and you will probably come across a place where someone was laid to rest. Everything you see in a burial ground is meant to be seen and, therefore, was probably thoughtfully chosen by either family or friends. In some instances the deceased may have selected their own grave markers. By the mid-1800s Illinoisans were able to choose from a wider variety of grave markings than previously available. Changing technology, job specialization, improved transportation from and communication with eastern states, and increased wealth all contributed to more consumer choice. Consequently, the markers chosen by Illinoisans reflected these broader social, economic, and technological changes. Also during this time period, the burial grounds on the east coast were undergoing change in layout. Eventually these changes, too, were evident in Illinois.

Burial grounds provide clues to changes across the landscape as well. Today, travelers on the back roads of Illinois frequently observe isolated burial grounds without a farmhouse, church, or community in view (1.15). These locations reflect changes that occurred over time. For example, regional economic development and population shifts may have caused changes in transportation systems; new roads were developed and old routes abandoned. Consequently, some early burial grounds that were originally located near roads may now be isolated and often forgotten. Similarly, early churches may have had a yard where congregants were buried. Over time, the church may have been relocated or torn down, resulting in a burial ground without an associated church building (1.16).

The social and cultural values held by individuals and communities reflect particular social and economic conditions. Changes in values, cultural institutions, economic conditions, and ethnic composition are reflected in the choices people make concerning the organization of burial grounds and the types of grave markers used to memorialize the dead. Thus, a burial ground and its markers are a window into the social and economic conditions of their time. Three examples illustrate this point. First, the shift from small family burial grounds to large, for-profit cemeteries shows that Americans transferred responsibility for burial from the family to commercial businesses in the mid- to late 1800s. In a second example, the shift from marble to granite grave markers at the end of the 1800s documents technological changes: the introduction of pneumatic tools enabled carving the harder granite, giving consumers a choice between the older marble styles or the modern granite styles. A third example is found when Caucasians and African Americans are buried in the same grounds that date to the mid-1800s, reminding us that not all communities adhered to the strict racial separation that was common prior to the Civil War.

We frequently associate burial grounds with genealogy. However, one need not know anyone in a burial ground to appreciate what can be learned there. Burial grounds and the items found within them are a focus of study by art historians, architects, folklorists, cultural geographers, archaeologists, anthropologists, and historians. Increasingly, burial ground studies are also the focus of people searching for ancestors, or nonspecialists interested in learning about the past or understanding the rituals of death.

When you visit a burial ground you are surrounded by, among other things, grave markers, fences, statues, and ornamental plantings. It is important to remember that in the beginning there was probably only a single grave. Thus, burial grounds should be viewed as dynamic places, much like farms and communities change over time.

Most burial grounds welcome visitors; everything you see in a burial ground was put there for the purpose of being seen by the living. Despite some decay, most everything you see informs you about the past. Our visits to burial grounds can be more rewarding when we remember that burial grounds and grave markers inform us not only about the individuals whose graves are marked but also about the society in which they lived. Your visit becomes more rewarding once you understand the different components of the burial ground.

When burial grounds are ignored, grave markers may be purposely damaged and destroyed or simply allowed to deteriorate. When this happens,

Fig. 1.15. Trees growing around an abandoned burial ground

Fig. 1.16. Churchyard burial ground and remnant of church

society loses an important part of what makes us who we are. Burial grounds are wonderful outdoor classrooms that can instill important lessons in history, art, and geology. Those who become familiar with the information contained in burial grounds are less likely to vandalize markers. Those who appreciate and respect burial grounds are more likely to support preservation efforts. In particular, this awareness is instrumental in saving burial grounds for future generations. We hope this guide will enrich your visits to burial grounds and inspire you to work toward their preservation.

CHAPTER 2
PREHISTORIC BURIAL GROUNDS

Prehistoric American Indians lived in Illinois for thousands of years, and archaeologists have documented their lifeways. In particular, they have studied the places where American Indians buried their dead. These include rock shelters (2.1), discrete burial areas in villages, isolated areas away from habitation sites, and prehistoric mounds (2.2). Both American Indians and later Illinoisans faced choices about where to bury their dead and how to mark the grave, choices based on who had died and who was responsible for the burial. Within each group of people, the preferred choices changed over time.

One type of prehistoric burial place—mounds—can sometimes be found within historical burial grounds. As such, these mounds warrant explanation so you may recognize them and understand their presence. Prehistoric burial mounds and historical burial grounds share two themes: both are places for burial of the dead and places for others to memorialize them. The main difference is the physical arrangement of the deceased.

Historical burial grounds in Illinois expanded horizontally below the ground, and individual graves were usually marked with a gravestone or other memorial. Graves were created in rows or family groups arranged horizontally (2.3), possibly reflecting conscious choices to bury family members close together.

In contrast, mounds expanded above the ground, both vertically and horizontally, over a long period of time. When someone died, the body was placed on the ground and covered with a small mound of earth. When the next person in the community died, the body was placed near the previous burial

Fig. 2.1. Modoc Rock Shelter, Randolph County

Fig. 2.2. Prehistoric burial mounds, Albany Mounds, Whiteside County

Fig. 2.3. Placement of markers showing rows of graves

Fig. 2.4. Starved Rock, Starved Rock State Park, La Salle County

and also covered with a small mound of earth. With each new burial, the mound would get wider and higher as people were buried above the ground. A mound is both a grave and a grave marker, though it may also have had some type of marker indicating individual or family burial locations.

Specific mounds may have been associated with family groups or clans, again possibly reflecting conscious choices to bury members close together. Over time, perhaps several generations or even several hundred years, mounds grew in size as more individuals were buried there. When a mound was no longer in use, prehistoric people may have "closed" the mound by capping it with special sediment (such as clay), and they may have performed special ceremonies.[1] A new mound would subsequently be created.

Mounds were just one method of burial practiced over time among the different American Indian groups. People have lived in Illinois for at least twelve millennia, and some of their practices existed for hundreds if not thousands of years. Documented European contact with American Indian people began in 1673, when French explorers visited the upper Illinois River valley at Starved Rock (2.4).

Prior to that contact, prehistoric peoples lived here much like early historical Illinois settlers. They raised families, built shelters and houses, hunted game, gathered wild foods, and later cultivated crops. People lived in single-family and extended family homes in both small and large communities. They also buried their dead.

Archaeologists have documented variation within the same prehistoric group as well as changes through time among various prehistoric cultures. For example, some peoples chose burial directly in the ground, others chose burial within a created mound, and still others exposed the remains to the elements for a natural process of decay. Once the remains became skeletons, the bones were gathered and buried in the ground. Finally, some peoples chose cremation as a burial practice, and often the cremains were buried. Although the manner in which we bury the dead differs through time, the common thread that has connected all cultures is a desire to bury our dead.

Archaeology and Burial Grounds

Archaeologists study and interpret patterns of past human behavior through their material culture (such as tools, pottery styles, house construction, and plant and animal remains) and through their mortuary practices, in particular the different places and manner of burial. To understand and explain these differences, archaeologists assign names descriptive of the cultural characteristics for each prehistoric and historical period. North American periods include the Archaic, the Woodland, and the Mississippian. These periods are subdivided into early, middle, and late because of the regional variations and technological advances documented within them. Among each of these groups, burial places vary as much as the people who created them.

Archaic

The Archaic (meaning old or ancient) period in Illinois encompasses the time period from approximately 10,000 to approximately 3,000 years ago. People of the time lived in small, mobile groups, traveling to different locations with the changing seasons. They relied on a hunting and gathering subsistence economy. Archaic places of burial reflected their seminomadic lifestyle. Burial locations varied among small mounds, natural rock shelters, and within villages, often in a river's floodplain or on nearby bluff tops. The practice of cremation also developed during this time. Early and Middle Archaic people buried the deceased in graves in shallow pits within or near village areas. Graves were both scattered and concentrated into discrete areas. Adult graves were sometimes marked with limestone slabs. Individuals of all ages and both sexes were interred in the same burial area, leading archaeologists to speculate that at some sites family groupings may have existed. Graves may have been marked in some manner or simply remembered.[2] This pattern is similar to how the early historical settlers in Illinois buried their dead.

Open-air sites, including rock shelters, contained graves in shallow pits within the habitation areas of a naturally occurring rock overhang. Toward the latter part of the Middle Archaic and into the Late Archaic, some burials were made near camps but others were some distance away on bluff tops in discrete concentrations of graves or in mounds. This shift in burial location reflected changes in lifestyle and regional variation in cultural traditions.[3] Some archaeologists believe that the deceased were not simply buried when they died but were held until a special ceremony could be performed at a particular place and a particular point in time. Moreover, these mobile groups likely carried remains back to established burial areas and at specific times.[4]

Woodland

The Woodland period was so named for the populations that lived in the eastern woodlands of the United States. In Illinois, the Woodland period ranges from approximately 3,000 to approximately 1,250 years ago. During this time, people shifted from a seminomadic existence to a more settled lifestyle, living in more permanent habitation or village areas and relying on domesticated and eventually cultivated plants. Larger groups of people began living together in concentrated areas.

Burial patterns in the Early Woodland continued from the Archaic period with the creation of mounds along bluff-top ridges overlooking streams or rivers. Mounds were typically oriented along the ridge contour and were associated with habitation sites. Some burials did occur within the villages. But these characteristics changed dramatically during the Middle Woodland period.

The Middle Woodland period is characterized by marked differences in social status as viewed through their material culture: increased tool production, intensification and expansion of trade networks, increased size, density, and complexity of populations, and increased reliance on cultivated native plant foods. Marked changes in this culture were also reflected in the manner of burial. Middle Woodland mounds were located both on bluff tops and in floodplains of major rivers (2.5) but seem to have been restricted to the central and lower Illinois River valleys. Some were large in size and contained specially prepared log tombs with a range of individuals present, from single to many interments. These tombs were likely used for many years and held individuals of all ages and both sexes, suggesting that the tombs were communal and served as family or clan burial plots.[5] However, not all Middle Woodland burials were in mounds. Some individuals were buried in discrete burial areas separate from villages. Differences in burial type and location, along with specific grave inclusions, indicate that this society was stratified, with clear distinctions between elite and common members. This pattern also occured during the historical period and will be discussed further in chapter 4.

The Middle Woodland culture abruptly ended approximately 1,800 years ago. The transition from Middle to Late Woodland was gradual; many of the characteristics remained as before but without the elaborate displays of exotic material. Hunting was still part of their subsistence base, but native plant cultivation became increasingly important. Settlements continued to grow

Fig. 2.5. Floodplain mound

Fig. 2.6. Bluff-top mound, Pere Marquette State Park, Jersey County

in size, prompting more reliance on cultivated plants and the introduction of maize (an early variety of corn), which could sustain a larger population size, thereby allowing people to remain in settled communities for longer periods of time.

Little archaeological documentation exists for Late Woodland burial practices in Illinois. We do know that burials were made in mounds primarily located on bluff tops (2.6) and occasionally in river floodplains. Discrete burial areas were also present and were associated with habitation sites. Both mounds and burial areas contained all ages and both sexes, but individuals had few grave artifacts with them. Charnel structures and cremations were also used. Charnel structures hold the remains of the deceased to allow for natural decay. After a period of time the bony remains were gathered together into a prepared bundle and buried, often in mounds. Archaeological evidence documents that Late Woodland burials were less elaborate, almost plain when compared to the Middle Woodland period.

Mississippian

The Mississippian period, named for the prehistoric populations who lived in the Mississippi River valley, developed from the local Late Woodland populations. The transition to Mississippian began 1,100 years ago and continued in Illinois until approximately 550 years ago. During the shift from Late Woodland to Early Mississippian, people lived in a variety of places including small family farmsteads, hamlets, and villages. Changes in tool technology, pottery styles, house construction, and community planning characterize the early Mississippian period. Also occurring at this time was the expansion of both local and long-distance trade networks, development of a ranked social society, and an intensification of maize agriculture. Early Mississippian burial practices included individual graves near or within houses, single and multiple interments in dedicated burial areas near habitation sites, bluff-top and floodplain mounds, and charnel structures. The practice of cremation also continued.

Between 700 and 900 years ago, populations began coalescing into small and large communities, bringing with them new ideas and technologies. Thus began the flourishing Middle Mississippian period. Earlier cultural and technological advances were greatly expanded and now included craft specialists, multiple episodes of mound construction, a calendar system (wood henges), and public works (mounds, ceremonial poles, and structures). Small and large communities were organized as planned communities with social and political control over a large population. There were distinct differences in social status and how people lived within the community. Elite members of Mississippian society controlled goods and services. They directed the construction of hundreds of earthen mounds, some for burial and some to support buildings, built around one or more open plazas that served as public spaces. Basic subsistence continued as before with hunting, fishing, and gathering of edible plant foods. However, one of the most significant changes in Mississippian lifeways was the intensification of and reliance on maize agriculture. Mississippians came to rely heavily on this grain, and it became their sustaining food source.

Researchers believe that smaller outlying towns supplied larger cities with food and goods necessary to maintain the population. Some archaeologists

Fig. 2.7. Mississippian mounds, Kincaid Mounds, Massac County

describe this transformation as a cultural "Big Bang."[6] Such drastic transformations have been intensively studied at the Cahokia site, located west of present-day Collinsville in St. Clair County, slightly north and east of St. Louis. Cahokia is viewed as a political, economic, and religious center that influenced other Mississippian towns across Illinois, southern Wisconsin, and the Southeast. Today the visible remnants of the site include eighty monumental earthworks. Similar changes also occurred at outlying Mississippian sites in Illinois, but to lesser degrees than at Cahokia.

Like other aspects of Mississippian life, mortuary practices were diverse. Burials occurred in isolated graves in or near homes, in separated burial areas near a community, in charnel structures, and in mounds. The use of stone box graves also began during this time. Limestone slabs lined the sides, bottom, and sometimes the top of the grave to create a stone box around the deceased. Mounds used for burial were located on nearby bluff tops and occasionally in the floodplain (2.7).

During the Middle Mississippian period, mortuary practices changed dramatically. Elite members were given preferential treatment in how and where they were buried. They were interred within specific burial mounds and prepared burial areas. These mounds were associated with the community but did not include common people. Elites' manner of burial was elaborate and included many grave objects, such as arrow points, shell beads and pendants, copper items, pipes, rattles, tools, and items of personal adornment. Nonelite members were buried in isolated graves or in a community burial area. Sometimes an object was placed with them, but not to the same degree as the elite. Thus, Mississippians clearly made conscious choices in where and how to bury their dead, and a person's role in life reflected his or her manner of burial. We see much the same distinction in historical burial grounds, where individuals who had an ordinary life have common burials but community leaders who enjoyed elevated social status have elaborate burials with distinct grave markers.

Later Prehistory

During the later periods of Illinois's prehistory, people settled into more permanent locations. Their chosen places of burial were in mounds or in burial areas near their villages. The increased amount of settlement may have provided them with a sense of place, establishing roots, if you will. Part of this settling down included a place to bury their dead in a location used through several generations. Just like their living places grew in size, their mounds and burial areas grew in number and size too. For example, a village may have had more than one burial mound associated with it. Some of the burial mounds are located high on the bluff tops overlooking a river.

Links to Modern Burial Grounds

In summary then, since the earliest people have lived in Illinois, there are two common themes in how the dead were treated. One is that they were usually buried in the ground. The other is that graves were often placed high on the landscape or near a source of flowing water—sometimes both. For many prehistoric peoples, graves were in burial mounds. Mounds' locations on high bluff tops and overlooking streams and rivers suggests that they were meant to be seen by people traveling up and down these waterways. Where we bury our dead now mirrors this pattern. Historical burial grounds are usually on high ground and are almost always near a source of water. In fact, several modern cemeteries have prehistoric mounds within them, illustrating continuity through time in how the burial of the dead occurs on the landscape.

Changes in settlement and subsistence patterns correlated with changes in burials. As prehistoric people became more settled and moved less often, burial grounds became more formal and were used over a longer period of time. Archaeologists can use observations of a mound's size, shape, and location to interpret its possible age and use pattern without excavation. This is similar to what we do when visiting historical burial grounds and observing the differences in grave markers and the layout of the burial ground itself.

Concern about preserving historical burial grounds should extend to prehistoric burial grounds as well so these important resources may be saved for future generations. Understanding prehistoric mounds and appreciating their meaning will, we hope, provide you with a stronger feeling for the past.

Visiting Prehistoric Burial Mounds

There are several locations in Illinois where prehistoric mounds are preserved as public parks and recreation areas (appendix A). In northwestern Illinois, you can visit the Dunleith Mound Group in East Dubuque's Gramercy Park, the John Chapman site and the Wapello Land and Water Reserve, both near the village of Hanover in Jo Daviess County, and the Albany Mounds near Albany (2.2) and the Sinnissippi Mounds in Sterling's Sinnissippi Park, both in Whiteside County. In northeastern Illinois are the Beattie Park Mound Group in Rockford's Beattie Park and the Briscoe Mounds near the village of Channahon in Will County (2.8). In west-central Illinois, you'll find Indian Mounds Park and Parker Heights Park, both in Quincy (2.9), and the Dickson Mounds State Park and the Ogden-Fettie Mound (2.10) near Lewistown in Fulton County. West of Collinsville and east of St. Louis is the Cahokia Mounds State Historic Site, which has over eighty prehistoric mounds. Pere Marquette State Park, near Grafton and the confluence of the Illinois and Mississippi Rivers, also has many prehistoric mounds. In far southern Illinois, Kincaid Mounds, southeast of Metropolis, also offers an opportunity to visit a large Mississippian mound site.

Fig. 2.8. Briscoe Mounds, Will County

In addition, prehistoric mounds can be found in some modern cemeteries. In the northern part of the state are Lost Mound Cemetery (2.11) south of Hanover and Oakwood Mound in Joliet's Oakwood Cemetery (2.12). In west-central Illinois, multiple mounds are visible in Quincy's Woodland Cemetery. In Greene County, a prehistoric mound is present in the Dayton Cemetery (2.13) south of Eldred.

Fig. 2.9. Indian Mounds Park, Adams County

Fig. 2.10. Ogden-Fettie Mound, Fulton County

Fig. 2.11. Prehistoric mound in Lost Mound Cemetery, Jo Daviess County

Fig. 2.12. Oakwood Mound, Oakwood Cemetery, Will County

Fig. 2.13. Prehistoric mound in Dayton Cemetery, Greene County

CHAPTER 3
COMMON FEATURES OF BURIAL GROUNDS

For many visitors, a trip to a burial ground means gathering around the grave of a loved one during a funeral. At those times we are probably unaware of our surroundings. On other occasions, when we are not participating in a burial, we are more likely to notice different types of grave markers, fences around family plots, roads, gates, and buildings. Since the early 1800s, when the first recognizable burial grounds appeared in Illinois, their appearance has continued to change. In one you may see only headstones and prairie flowers, while in another you may encounter fences, roads, buildings, or a virtual forest of trees.

This chapter describes what you can expect to see in a burial ground. The first part of the chapter focuses on headstones and is organized chronologically, around the raw materials used in their manufacture. We take this approach because the transition from one type of material to another informs us about broader social and technological changes that were taking place. The second part of the chapter goes beyond the grave markers to explore other material components of burial grounds, including family plots, roads, buildings, and gates.

In the first third of the nineteenth century, settlement in Illinois occurred primarily in rural settings, as there were few villages and towns. Burial and memorialization was a family responsibility. The family prepared the body for burial, dug the grave, and buried the individual. If family was not available, close friends may have performed these tasks. Before stonemasons were available, the family probably marked the grave with wood or locally available fieldstone.

Fig. 3.1. Uninscribed sandstone marker

Fig. 3.2. Sandstone marker roughly shaped and inscribed by an amateur

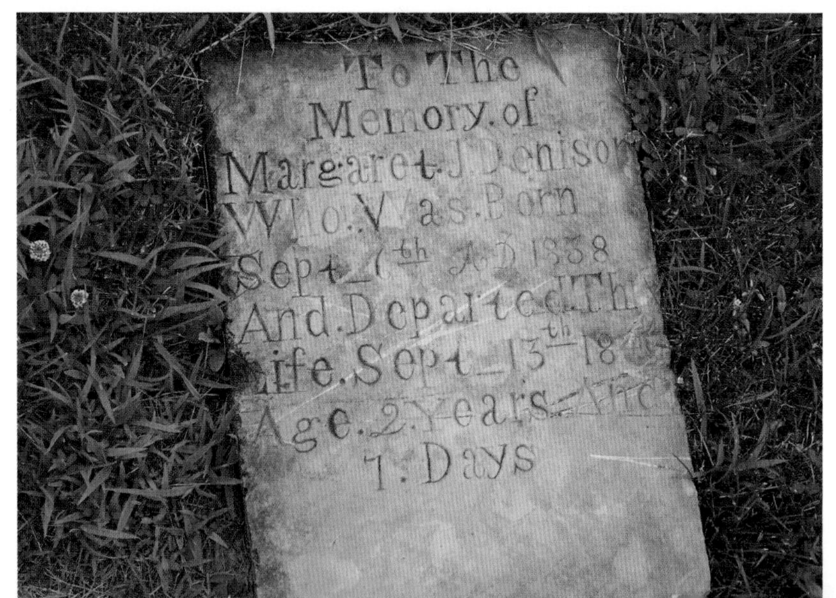

Fig. 3.3. Professionally inscribed sandstone marker

Fig. 3.4. Professionally inscribed epitaph on sandstone marker

As you explore burial grounds, you will see that many of the unshaped markers are not inscribed (3.1), possibly due to a high illiteracy rate. The rarity of professional stone carvers probably contributes to rough shapes and haphazard inscriptions (3.2). If the service of a stonemason was available, the family may have had the stone shaped and inscribed with the deceased's name as well as the dates of birth and death (3.3). A motif or epitaph might also be included (3.4).

By the mid-1800s, as the population congregated into towns and villages and the commercial population expanded, professional stonemasons and eventually full-service mortuary and monument businesses became commonplace across Illinois. Improvements in communication with and transportation to the eastern United States expanded the options for the types of material used for grave markers, the design of the stone, and the motifs and epitaphs applied.

Marking the Grave

The most common item found in burial grounds is the grave marker. The marker has several roles. It identifies the grave, memorializes the deceased, and enables the living and the dead to interact. Most people's lives attract little public recognition and do not warrant inclusion in history books or even newspapers. The grave marker provides a degree of public recognition for those who otherwise may go unnoticed.

The original intent behind the placing of a grave marker may remain unknown. We may confidently conclude that it provides an unmistakable visual connection between the dead and a specific location on the landscape. As such, the marker is also sending a message to the living: Someone is buried here, not someplace else. We know this because the marker tells us so. "Here lies" is quite specific as to where the body is located. "Sacred to the Memory of" carved atop a marker is a clear message that the marker conveys important meaning for the living. The grave marker represents a way to remember a life that has passed. For some, it may also give details of a person's life—where they were from and what they may have done during their lives. For others, dates of birth and death are all we learn.

Markers are placed for family members, for friends, and for strangers (for example, unknown soldiers). They might represent the last physical link to someone now gone. While a person may have had an ordinary life, his or her passing creates a void. The marker is a reminder that the life had meaning. The marker also helps with grief and the transition associated with a loved one's passing. As such, it identifies a place to return to time and again, where one can leave flowers, pebbles, or coins as a sign of visitation and remembrance. In most instances, grave markers reflect the thoughts and beliefs of the survivors. There are instances, however, when the deceased left instructions on how the grave marker should be designed.

It is fair to say that almost everything we see in a burial ground was placed there for the living. These include headstones (3.5), enclosures (3.6), sculptures (3.7), and mausoleums (3.8). Depending on the type of burial ground, you may see some or all of these items. These elements reflect the age and location of the burial ground as well as the social and economic status of both the deceased and those responsible for the marking.

Headstones are the most common way to mark a grave. In New England, these markers date back to the 1600s. In Illinois, grave markers have a much shorter history. Euro-Americans and their descendants did not officially reach Illinois until the arrival of French explorers in the mid- to late 1600s, and full-time settlements were not established until the late 1700s. Large towns and cities did not develop in Illinois until the 1830s and 1840s.

Researchers studying New England grave markers have documented the "Puritan way of death" that was common in the 1600s or 1700s.[1] The Puritans had a harsh view of death, lacked sentimentality, and discouraged placing religious symbols on markers. Death heads, scythes, and hourglasses are common, while crosses and other religious motifs are absent. The authors have not observed any death heads or scythes on markers in Illinois, no doubt because of the generally later settlement of Illinois. The earliest grave markers in Illinois date to the early 1800s, and migrants to Illinois would have brought the more contemporary gravestone designs with them. By then the "Puritan way of death" had been replaced in the eastern states by a less harsh view of death that developed during the Great Awakening of the mid-1700s. Death

Fig. 3.5. Various headstones

Fig. 3.6. Family plot with coping

Fig. 3.7. Marble sculpture

Fig. 3.8. Mausoleum

head images changed into "soul effigies," sometimes referred to as cherubs. The urn and the willow tree appeared by the 1800s.[2] These and other iconographic images are discussed in chapter 5.

Headstones

In Illinois, headstones are made from a variety of materials. Most likely, the ones you see will be made from sandstone (3.9), limestone (3.10), marble (3.11), granite (3.12), concrete (3.13), or zinc (3.14). Occasionally, you may also encounter markers carved from wood (3.15) or slate (3.16) or formed from iron (3.17).

The types of stone found naturally in Illinois were limited to primarily sandstone and, to a lesser extent, limestone. These materials were used extensively in burial grounds during the first half of the nineteenth century. Marble and granite do not occur naturally in Illinois, but they are common materials for grave markers after the 1850s because of improved transportation from quarries in the eastern and southern United States. Despite some temporal overlap, the use of local stones was mostly replaced by marble in the 1850s. In turn, marble was replaced by granite around 1900. We explore these changes below.

Many of the most common styles of grave markers were carved out of different raw materials. Appendix B, Marker Geology, will help you identify the various types of raw materials used. Appendix C, Marker Styles Common in Illinois, is a photographic key of the different marker styles and provides a broad representation of what you can expect to see when you visit burial grounds in Illinois.

Fig. 3.9. Sandstone marker

Fig. 3.10. Limestone marker

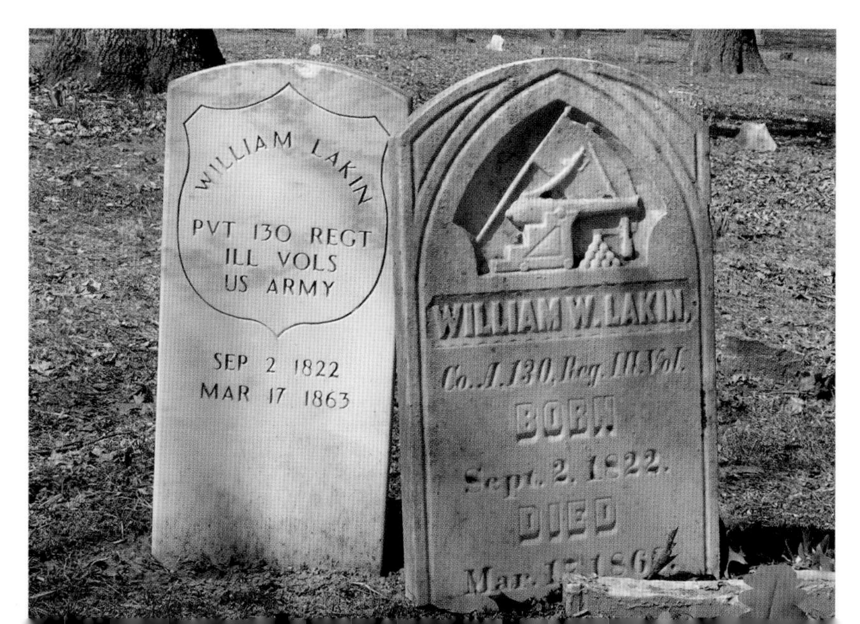

Fig. 3.11. Marble marker

Fig. 3.12. Granite marker

Fig. 3.13. Concrete marker

Fig. 3.14. Zinc marker

Fig. 3.15. Wooden marker

Fig. 3.16. Slate marker

Fig. 3.17. Iron marker

Design

All simple headstones made from sandstone, limestone, slate, and marble have a similar appearance (3.18). The top may or may not have a design (see appendix C); underneath the top there may be an image, followed by the name of the deceased, family position (husband, wife, son, or daughter), and then the dates for birth and/or death. If an epitaph is used, it is placed under the death date. Finally, the carver's name might appear, located below all the other inscriptions and either to the left, or more commonly, to the right (3.19).

Fig. 3.18. The headstone of Job Mathis illustrates the general style of tablet markers

Orientation

The placement of the body relative to the marker changed over time. As a general rule, sandstone, limestone, slate, and marble tablet (rectangular) markers have the inscription facing west with the body behind the marker facing east toward the rising sun, a placement associated with the Christian idea of the resurrection. European Iron Age bodies were also placed with the head to the west and feet to the east, facing the day's first light. Later Christians did the same since the second coming of Christ was associated with the rising sun.[3] In contrast, granite markers usually face east with the body also facing east. Thus, when reading a tablet sandstone, slate, or marble marker, you are not likely standing on the grave, but when reading a granite marker, there is a good chance that you are. There are exceptions, however. It is a good idea to check the orientation of other markers in the cemetery

Fig. 3.19. Carver's name inscribed on bottom of marker

as well as the condition of the grass as a clue to the grave's location (3.20). On a flat surface, tablet markers may begin to tilt toward the grave (3.21), but on a slope, gravity may cause tilting away from the grave. Many headstones predating the use of granite and concrete (before circa 1900) are also accompanied by a smaller footstone (3.22) that was placed at the foot end of the grave. Thus, the grave is located between the two markers. Footstones are typically inscribed with the individual's initials.

In the 1800s, husbands and wives usually had their own marble markers and were buried in a manner similar to their position in the marriage ceremony. During the ceremony the husband is on the left from the clergy's point of view. The inscription on marble markers usually face west. However, the bodies in the grave face east. Therefore, since the markers face west, when you read the inscription for husband and wife on marble markers, the inscription for

Fig. 3.20. Grass pattern indicating location of graves

Fig. 3.21. Leaning markers

Fig. 3.22. Sandstone head and foot markers

Fig. 3.23. Cenotaph

Fig. 3.24. Marker for a leg

the wife is to the left of the husband's. By the 1900s, a single granite marker was used for both the husband and wife. Since granite markers usually face east, the inscription for the wife is to the right of the husband's inscription.

One unique marker is the cenotaph (3.23), a marker for a person buried elsewhere. In some instances a marker may acknowledge only a portion of a body (3.24).

The types of headstone markers prevalent in historical burial grounds in Illinois are discussed in more detail below. The order follows the general chronology for when each material first appeared in Illinois. Following that is a brief discussion on other types of structures.

Materials

WOOD Professional gravestone carvers were rare in Illinois during the first third of the nineteenth century. In addition, suitable stone that could be quarried and used for headstones was not available in the state. There were no community-based monument dealers until the mid-1800s. Thus, many early graves were probably marked with wood or may not have been marked at all. Memorializing a loved one or friend may have been as simple as erecting a small wooden plank, which could have been fashioned into a marker quickly. The marker might have included a name and possibly the dates of birth and death. If a cross was desired, it might be either carved into the wood or fashioned from the wood. It is unclear if epitaphs were included since no wood markers from the early 1800s have been documented. If an epitaph was desired and someone was skilled enough to do the carving, it is more likely that a stone would have been used rather than wood because the stone would have lasted longer. Many burial grounds have open areas possibly indicating where there are unmarked burials (3.25). We see clusters of marble and granite markers, but these clusters surround areas without any markers. The absence of markers in many early burial grounds is no doubt due to the decay of wood markers and the subsequent decision not to replace them with stone. Another possibility is that some graves never had a marker, but it is more likely that the graves were marked with wood. Since wood in contact with soil is prone to deterioration, it is doubtful that any early wood markers survive in Illinois. However, wood markers from the 1900s do survive. For example, Carrie Etta Pech's marker from 1937 is held above the ground by pipes (3.26).

FIELDSTONE Fieldstone refers to local sandstone or limestone minimally shaped and usually not inscribed (3.27). These stones almost always represent early graves and are frequently located in the center of a burial ground where later markers are also present, though there can be instances where they occur later—the lack of inscription can make it difficult to judge the date. The absence of monument dealers during the early 1800s in Illinois usually meant that when stone was used, it was restricted to what was locally available. The high level of illiteracy in that period likely contributes to the lack of inscriptions. An illiterate family would have been unable to inscribe the stone with messages of remembrance (names, dates, and epitaph). It is also possible that even if a family was literate, a lack of technical skills and proper tools and the absence of professional stone carvers may have affected

Fig. 3.25. Absence of markers where graves are probably located

Fig. 3.26. Wooden marker for Carrie Etta Pech

the ability to have the stone inscribed. Finally, family and friends may have simply chosen to leave markers plain.

Some fieldstone grave markers are also accompanied by a footstone. These smaller, rough-cut stones are usually placed at the foot of the grave, typically within six feet of the headstone. Because they were minimally shaped and often not inscribed, it is likely that both head- and footstones were placed at the grave soon after burial.

Keep in mind that many early settlers came from areas with a long tradition of marking graves with both simple and elaborately carved headstones.

Fig. 3.27. Rough-cut sandstone marker without inscription

The Illinois frontier lacked the carvers and stones previously available. Thus, the lack of well-crafted headstones is a function of circumstance and not necessarily of choice.

SANDSTONE Sandstone is widely available in some portions of Illinois, but its presence is geographically restricted. As a result, sandstone markers are mostly found in southern and central Illinois. In addition, those sections of the state were settled first. By the time the northern section was settled in greater numbers, marble was becoming available.

When used for grave markers, quarried sandstone usually exhibits saw or chisel marks along the sides (3.28). Some stones may also show marks used to guide the shaping of the stone (3.29). We have never seen a shaped sandstone marker that did not also contain some type of inscription (3.30). Because sandstone was readily available, we believe that sandstone markers were probably inscribed soon after death. Some sandstone markers contain designs and images similar to those found in burial grounds outside Illinois.

The discoid-shaped markers (3.31) from the Livingston Cemetery in Clark County share a unique style documented in states southeast and southwest of Illinois.[4] More prevalent are markers that have either rounded (3.32) or flat (3.33) shoulders, styles reflective of the eastern colonial states.[5] Sandstone ledgers atop box tombs (3.34) and columns (3.35) are also present though less common.

Several inscriptions that first appeared in eastern states and were later brought to Illinois include "Sacred to the Memory of" (3.36), "In Memory of," and "consort" (referring to a wife or occasionally a husband; 3.37). Additionally, motifs common to older markers in eastern states included winged

Fig. 3.28. Saw marks on a sandstone marker

Fig. 3.29. Sandstone marker with inscribed lines to assist carver in shaping

Fig. 3.30. Ovoid-shaped sandstone marker with rough inscription

Fig. 3.31. Multiple ovoid sandstone markers

Fig. 3.32. Sandstone marker with round shoulders

Fig. 3.33. Sandstone marker with flat shoulders

Fig. 3.34. Sandstone box tomb

Fig. 3.35. Sandstone column

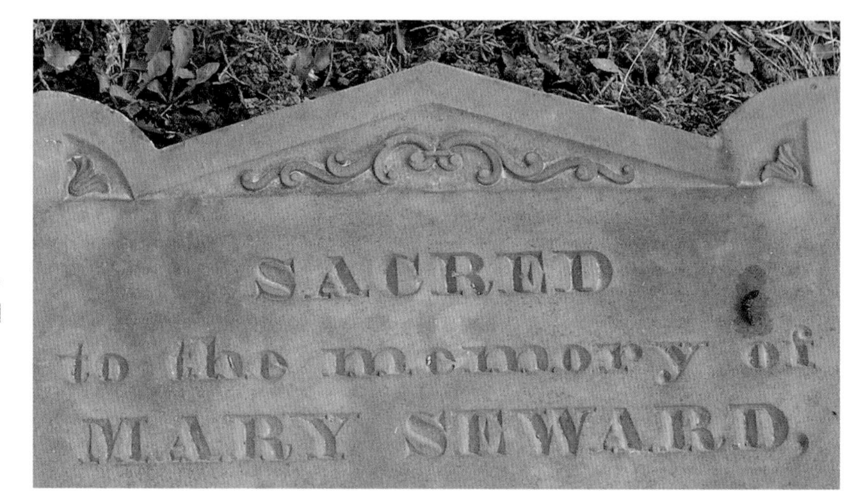

Fig. 3.36. Sandstone marker with "Sacred to the memory of" inscription

Fig. 3.37. "Consort" inscribed on sandstone marker

Fig. 3.38. Winged cherub motif inscribed on sandstone marker

Fig. 3.39. Urn motif inscribed on sandstone marker

cherubs (3.38), urns (3.39), and willow trees (3.40). In the eastern United States there was a chronological order to inscriptions and images. Because Illinois was settled later, these various inscriptions and images appeared here simultaneously. In addition, local Illinois carvers applied their own talents. The folk art and stylized inscriptions found on many sandstone markers are examples of the individuality expressed by local carvers (3.41).

This emphasis on individual creativity in the early to mid-1800s contrasts with the widespread similarity in styles that characterizes markers from the latter half of the 1800s.

Fig. 3.40. Willow tree inscribed on sandstone marker

Fig. 3.41. Folk art inscribed on shoulder of sandstone marker

In the eastern United States, researchers study the fonts and motifs specific to the carver.[6] Unfortunately, in Illinois the carvers of sandstone markers did not always put their names on the stone. Some of these early carvers did (3.42), but their work is not well documented. It is a good assumption the early Illinois carvers of sandstone markers probably did not have their products widely distributed across the state. For one thing, the transportation corridors in the first third of the nineteenth century were less developed than those in the eastern states. Second, the state's lower population density

Fig. 3.42. Carver's name inscribed on sandstone marker

also meant fewer opportunities for full-time carvers. In the late 1830s and early 1840s many stonemasons migrated to northern Illinois to work on the Illinois and Michigan Canal. However, there probably would not have been an opportunity for them to supplement their employment as gravestone carvers. German immigrants to Illinois brought with them a tradition of stone farmhouse and barn construction;[7] although there is no clear evidence, it is possible that some carved gravestones for family and friends. There is no doubt that highly skilled stonemasons carved gravestones in Illinois during the first half of the 1800s (3.43), but there is no evidence indicating that any of them worked full-time as carvers. This is in contrast with eastern carvers, who were full-time professionals, signed their work, and may have employed other carvers.[8] It is more likely that early stonemasons in Illinois combined activities associated with stonemasonry (building construction and production of millstones and gravestones).

Despite their skills, even professional carvers did make mistakes, now preserved in burial grounds. In one example (3.44), the carver ran out of room, and the last *t* in the name was placed above it.

In the latter half of the century, as marble became more widely available in Illinois, sandstone is still often used for bases since sandstone was less expensive and was still locally available. The popularity of using sandstone for grave markers greatly declined in the mid-1800s due to consumer preference for marble. Still, some sandstone headstones date to the late 1800s (3.45).

SLATE Slate markers are common in the northeastern United States. In Illinois, slate suitable for grave markers is not readily available, and slate markers are not common. During the early 1800s, several carvers did make

Fig. 3.43. Complex anthropomorphic carving on sandstone marker

Fig. 3.44. Carver's mistake on sandstone marker

Fig. 3.45. Sandstone grave marker with date of 1875

markers from slate quarried in Indiana.[9] Several burial grounds along the Wabash River are good candidates for containing slate markers. One of the best locations is the Sand Hill Cemetery in Mount Carmel, Wabash County.

MARBLE In Illinois, marble was the dominant material in the manufacture of grave markers in the last half of the 1800s. Since marble was worked with hand tools, its softness made it easy to shape. Unfortunately, it also weathers poorly and is susceptible to the damaging effects of wind, rain, and pollution. As a result, many marble markers are now difficult to read.

In New England, sandstone and slate markers, resistant to weathering, abundant in supply, and with a long history of use, are the focus of researchers and burial-ground enthusiasts. In contrast, marble markers in that region do not attract the same interest, probably due to their poor weathering qualities and relative sameness in style. In Illinois, however, marble markers are abundant compared to sandstone markers, making them a focus of attention and study despite their sometimes poor condition.

Although marble and granite are the most popular stones present in Illinois burial grounds, there are no quarries for them in Illinois. These stones were not available until the arrival of the railroads in the mid-1800s. When marble did become available, it quickly replaced sandstone as the primary stone used for grave markers. Marble's popularity represented a convergence of improved transportation, growing consumerism, evolving religious sentiment, and an increased desire for expressing wealth and status in death. The use of marble profoundly affected how burial grounds looked (see chapter 4). Sandstone markers frequently included images of folk art and often showcased the styles of local carvers. These local sandstone traditions were short-lived, replaced with marble carving using national styles gleaned from catalogs. The marble styles were mass-produced, and their popularity is believed to have reflected consumers' desire to be associated with the "new" product. Marble marker styles and shapes in Illinois are similar to marble markers found in Ohio, Indiana, and other nearby states. Designs and images are no longer attributable to a specific carver. Sentimental themes reflecting loss are dominant in the motifs. These themes are closely associated with the Victorian Period of Death (see chapter 5).

Marble was quarried in Vermont starting in 1785, and by the 1840s the Rutland marble quarries were in full operation.[10] Local railroads and canals made marble accessible throughout the northeast, Pennsylvania, and Ohio. However, transport to Illinois was delayed until the 1850s, when railroads expanded across the state and linked Vermont to Illinois.[11] Prior to the railroads, the movement of marble to and within Illinois was not practical given its cost and weight.

Soon after the railroads arrive, we also see marble dealers and marble cutters in Illinois (3.46). Illinois census reports do not enumerate marble dealers, cutters, or factories until the 1860 census. Just as the early gravestone carvers from the eastern states used their skills to manufacture other items such as furniture, the Illinois marble dealers marketed a variety of products to the public—for example, fireplace mantels. The manufacturing technology for saws advanced to the point that cut marks seen on marble were more regular in appearance than saw cuts on the earlier sandstone (3.47; see also 3.28).

Once marble was available, it was marketed very effectively. Advertisements for grave markers mentioned only marble. Marble had become the new product in the funeral industry. When we examine death dates on markers,

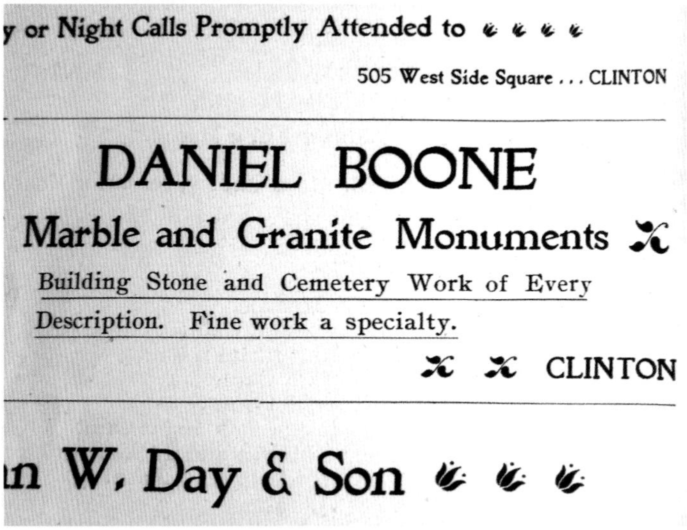

Fig. 3.46. Advertisement of marble dealer. Reproduced from *Clinton City Directory and DeWitt County Gazetteer*, 1899, compiled and printed by Daily and Weekly Public, Clinton, Illinois, 68.

Fig. 3.47. Saw marks on marble marker

we find a noticeable reduction in the use of sandstone after marble became available. Marble was highly desirable to merchants because of its ease in carving. Consumers were attracted to marble because it was a new product that offered motifs and designs not previously available. During the transition to marble, some families chose more traditional phrasing for the words on the marker. The use of "Sacred to the Memory of" and "consort of" are closely associated with sandstone markers but may occur on marble. The term "relict" (denoting widow) is also a term from an earlier time that is sometimes found on marble (3.48).

Marble is used for a variety of marker styles. Simple one-piece marble markers are probably the most common (3.49). These are usually accompanied by smaller footstones. Similar to sandstone footstones, the marble footstones are frequently inscribed with the initials of the deceased. The presence of marble footstones in burial grounds today is uncommon for a variety of reasons. Many were removed to facilitate mowing (3.50). Others fell down and were covered over time and now lie below the surface. In other instances, the footstones were taken as souvenirs.

The popularity and availability of marble led to a widespread practice of replacing older markers, originally made from wood or locally available stone, with marble. It is also possible that some marble markers were added to graves that did not previously have a marker. The easiest way to recognize replacement marble markers is to read the death date: replacement markers have death dates preceding the coming of the railroad. Thus, a marble marker with a death date of 1825 (3.51) could not have been carved in that year, since there would have been no place to obtain marble in Illinois at that time. Another good example is the marker for Abraham Lincoln's store partner from New Salem, Wm. F. Berry (3.52). The front of his marker has

Fig. 3.48. “Relict” inscribed on marble marker

Fig. 3.49. Simple marble tablet markers

Fig. 3.50. Stack of footstones removed from grave sites

Fig. 3.51. Replacement marble marker carved long after 1825

Figs. 3.52–3.53. Replacement marble marker for A. Lincoln's store partner, front and reverse

his personal information, while the back references his connection to Lincoln (3.53). Given the death date of 1835, the marker was replaced long after Berry's death when Lincoln became well-known. The use of marble as a replacement stone might reflect socioeconomic status because the cost of marble and the charge for inscribing the stone may have exceeded affordability for many. Thus, replacement markers may be a reflection of individual and community prosperity.

Beginning in the mid-1800s, archaeological investigations in the Mediterranean gave rise to a general interest in classical architecture, contributing to the popularity of marble. Simple markers evolved into larger and more elaborate monuments. As markers changed from simple to complex, there were more instances of markers that distinguished between adults and children. One of the more common child markers is a small obelisk (3.54). In contrast, adults have larger and more elaborate columns, including some with statues on top (3.55, 3.56).

The arched double column was used to illustrate family relationships. These include husband and wife, mother and father (3.57), mother and daughter, and siblings. Despite the inscribed death dates from the mid-1800s, these markers probably date to the late 1800s.

By the last quarter of the century, a different variety of marble was introduced. This gray-colored marble is used most commonly on columns (3.58) and is found in many larger cemeteries. Unfortunately, it does not weather well in Illinois. Many of these markers are faded and difficult to read.

Fig. 3.54. Child's obelisk, marble

Fig. 3.55. Large marble column atop a limestone base

Fig. 3.56. Large marble statue

Fig. 3.57. Arched double column of marble denoting family relationships

Fig. 3.58. Late-nineteenth-century gray marble column

LIMESTONE Depending on what part of the state you are in, you may come across tablet markers made from locally available limestone. These markers share many of the characteristics of sandstone and marble headstones (3.59). Not until you are up close is it apparent that they are made from limestone (see appendix B). They may mark graves from as early as the first third of the 1800s. When marble became available, there was a reduction in the use of limestone for tablet markers.

Beginning in the late 1800s and continuing into the early 1900s we see distinctive limestone markers made primarily from material imported from

Fig. 3.59. Limestone tablet marker

the Bedford quarries in Indiana.[12] Well suited for carving, this soft limestone was used to make sculptures in a rustic art form, rather than for the simpler tablet markers. The rustic style, which began in the late 1700s, reflects natural themes. Originally the rustic style was applied to furniture, silverware, ceramics, and picture frames. Its use on grave markers around the turn of the century was a rejection of the mourning motifs common to the Victorian style applied to marble markers (see chapter 5). Popular examples include tree trunks (3.60), logs, chairs, and pulpits (3.61). Tree trunks usually have a portion of the bark peeled back, with the names and dates of the deceased inscribed (3.62). Other popular themes included twigs (3.63), branches, leaves (3.64), vines, tools (3.65), and occasionally wildlife (3.66). The similarity of these limestone sculptures marking graves throughout Illinois demonstrates the influence of rail transportation, widening consumer choice, and the popularity of the rustic style, examples of which were illustrated in dealer catalogs of the era. The customer now had a wider choice beyond the ubiquitous marble.

The complex rustic images were usually carved on recently quarried, softer material because the longer the limestone remained unmodified, the harder it became. In addition, the reduced weight of a carved stone made it cheaper to ship long-distance. Because they were usually carved outside the state, these markers do not contain a carver's name. Throughout Illinois one can see the variety of styles made from limestone. These styles are somewhat unique to limestone, not duplicated in other stone materials.

One interesting type of limestone marker is the "World War I" soldier statue. This marker is very detailed, showing components of the uniform as well as tree stumps adjacent to the soldier (3.67 and 3.68). The Bohemian National Cemetery in Chicago has one of the largest collections of limestone sculptures in Illinois, many depicting "World War I" soldiers.

Fig. 3.60. Elaborate limestone tree sculpture

Fig. 3.61. Limestone pulpit

Fig. 3.62. Limestone tree trunk with bark "peeled" off to expose inscription

Fig. 3.63. Limestone sculptured twigs

Fig. 3.64. Limestone sculptured leaves

Fig. 3.65. Limestone sculptured hammer

Fig. 3.66. Limestone sculptured squirrel

Limestone statues were not limited to "World War I" soldiers; images of other people were also carved. The markers for Alexander and Margaret Partridge in the Sand Ridge Cemetery in Woodford County are unique (3.69). They were carved by well-known sculptor John Petarde from Peoria.

More common are the limestone tree stumps associated with the Modern Woodmen of America (MWA) and the Woodmen of the World (WOW) organizations. The symbol of the MWA, which began in 1883, is an ax, mallet, and sedge on a shield (3.70). The WOW formed as a breakaway organization in 1890. Its symbol is a circle with a tree stump in the center and the

Fig. 3.67. Limestone sculptured World War I soldier

Fig. 3.68. Detail of soldier's belt

organization's initials or name around the circle (3.71). Both organizations began as a way for members to afford the cost of funerals.[13] The decline in the use of these limestone sculptures by the 1930s probably reflects changing consumer interest.

ZINC A distinctive metal marker found throughout north and central Illinois, though rare in southern Illinois, is the bluish-gray metal marker (3.72) commonly referred to as white bronze.[14] The metal is actually a zinc alloy. It is cast in molds to form hollow markers (3.73) and statues reminiscent of the

Fig. 3.69. Limestone sculpture for Alexander and Margaret Partridge

Fig. 3.70. Modern Woodmen of America symbol

Fig. 3.71. Woodmen of the World symbol

Fig. 3.72. Zinc / "white bronze" statue

Fig. 3.73. View within zinc marker exposing hollow core

styles previously etched in both marble and granite. The surface is sandblasted to give the granular appearance of stone. The bluish-gray color forms when the zinc is exposed to the air and transformed into zinc carbonate.

The column is the most common form for zinc markers. It features plaque inserts for each of the four sides. Other forms include statues, bedsteads, tablets, raised plaques, and lawn-level plaques (3.74, 3.75, and 3.76). Zinc markers were manufactured by one company, the Monumental Bronze Company of Bridgeport, Connecticut. In addition to the foundry in Connecticut, the company had several subsidiaries in Chicago, Detroit, and Des Moines (3.77). Local agents sold the markers, and selections were made from examples already in a cemetery or from a catalog. Many markers did not display the manufacturer's name, but some marker bases carry the subsidiary's name: the American Bronze Company, American White Bronze Company, Detroit Bronze Company, or Western White Bronze Company. Zinc markers were advertised as cheaper and more durable alternatives to marble and granite. Zinc was also seen as a more progressive material in an age when industrialization and consumerism were on the rise.

Most of these markers were commissioned in the 1880s and 1890s. Technological changes in the processing of the zinc enabled the manufacturer to mass-produce hollow statues. The statues were no longer manufactured after 1914, with the beginning of World War I, but the company did continue to produce tablets and plaques for family members. If you are uncertain whether a marker is made from zinc or iron, try placing a magnet on it. The magnet will not adhere to zinc.

Many burial grounds in Illinois have one or two zinc markers. A few burial grounds, such as the Pontiac City Cemetery in Pontiac (Livingston County) and the Oakland Cemetery in Princeton (Bureau County), have twenty or more examples each.

IRON Other metal grave markers are not common but do occur. Most probably date to the late 1800s and early 1900s. These can be in the form of cast-iron grave cover (3.78) or wrought iron (3.79). In 1887, James K. P. Shelton of Sumter County, Alabama, patented a design that held an insert for the deceased's birth and death dates. There might also be a space for a photograph.[15] The marker could have a glass cover placed over the insert, or the information could be painted directly on the metal (3.80). This particular style has been observed in only a few Illinois burial grounds. Another style of metal marker was the iron cross. The iron cross marker might also include porcelain insets for the name (3.81 and 3.82). One interesting wrought-iron marker (3.83) is in the Lakeside Cemetery in Tazewell County. The unique design is repeated in the footstone.

Fig. 3.74. Zinc bedstead

Fig. 3.75. Zinc plaque

Fig. 3.76. Zinc lawn-level marker

Fig. 3.77. The mark of zinc manufacturer American White Bronze Co., Chicago

Fig. 3.78. Cast-iron grave cover

Fig. 3.79. Iron cross

Fig. 3.80. Iron tablet with place for insert containing information about the deceased

Fig. 3.81. Iron cross with porcelain insert

Fig. 3.82. Close-up of porcelain insert

Fig. 3.83. Elaborate wrought-iron marker

GRANITE As with most other materials discussed, the use of granite in Illinois burial grounds occurs long after its appearance in the eastern states. Improved transportation and technology after the Civil War allowed quarry operators in New England to expand the market for granite. By the early 1900s, granite quarries were even open in Georgia. Specifically, improvements in cranes enabled the lifting and maneuvering of the heavier granite. The carving of sandstone, marble, and limestone had been done with chisels and mallets, a difficult and inefficient process on the harder granite. The introduction of pneumatic tools allowed the harder material to be carved economically and allowed for deeper incisions into the stone.[16]

Granite appears in Illinois burial grounds at the end of the 1800s and beginning of the 1900s. Its introduction reflected changing consumer habits driven by monument companies' effective marketing practices. Granite markers were widely available from local dealers as well as through Sears and Montgomery Ward catalogs (3.84).

With the shift away from marble, there was a change in marker color and style. Granite offered the consumer a range of colors (reds and grays) beyond the ubiquitous white marble. The earliest granite markers displayed rounded pillows or logs (3.85). The inscriptions were very shallow and may have reflected the lack of pneumatic tools. Other early granite markers also

Fig. 3.84. Grave marker catalog from Montgomery Ward

Fig. 3.85. Early granite pillow or log marker

Fig. 3.86. Shallow carving on an early granite marker

Fig. 3.87. Deeper carving on a later granite marker

Fig. 3.88. Early granite marker for husband and wife

Fig. 3.89. Arched double column for family members using both granite and marble

had shallow inscriptions (3.86). As pneumatic tools became the norm, the depth of the inscriptions increased (3.87).

Many of the early granite markers were larger and more squared than the previous marble markers. While the simple marble markers were usually for a single person, granite markers frequently were for both husband and wife (3.88). Granite was also incorporated into the marble double-column arched markers prominent during the late 1800s (3.89). Eventually, granite replaced marble for column markers (3.90). As cemetery designs changed (see chapter 4), granite markers were set lower to the ground (3.91).

Fig. 3.90. Granite column

Fig. 3.91. Granite ground marker

Fig. 3.92. Granite replacement marker

Like marble markers, granite was used for some replacement markers. Given that granite was not available in Illinois until around 1900, a granite marker with a death date of 1865 was definitely made long after the death (3.92).

Today, granite continues to be the prominent stone used in cemeteries.

CONCRETE You may occasionally see concrete markers. Most are small and contain brief inscriptions of names and dates (3.93). Concrete markers are usually simple in design and lack epitaphs, motifs, or special designs. However, occasionally more elaborate concrete markers may be observed (3.94). At first, one might conclude that concrete was chosen because it was inexpensive (which it was) and did not require a professional stone carver (which it may not have). While this might be true in most instances, there may be another reason for selecting concrete.

By the early 1900s, Illinois farmers were increasingly using concrete for barn floors, house foundations, and walkways. Various early twentieth-century guides instructed farmers on the best way to position and construct the various buildings needed on a prosperous farm. These books touted the utility and benefits of concrete as a building material. Farmers, who were among the earliest users of concrete, may be viewed as being progressive for the use of this new building material. It is reasonable to conclude that for some, the use of concrete as a grave marker represented an extension of its use on the farm. It would be a mistake to simply conclude that the presence of a concrete marker was a reflection of either poverty or low social status. It is also likely that concrete represented a closer connection between the living and the dead since either a family member or friend may have created the marker. Thus, the use of concrete (a new building material) to make a grave marker can be interpreted as a sign of being progressive.

Military Markers

During the Civil War, the federal government assumed the role of burying the war's dead (see chapter 4). Originally, grave markers were made from wood. However, by 1873 the cost of periodically replacing wood markers was judged too costly. Consequently, marble replaced wood. The Rutland marble quarries in Vermont manufactured over 250,000 markers, which were shaped by machines. Iron sheets covered portions of the stone. Areas not covered were sand blasted, leaving the person's name and regiment in relief.[17]

Two types of Civil War markers were made. The earliest version is tall and slim (3.95), while the later version is shorter and wider (3.96). Both have a slightly curved top. When issued by the government, the markers listed only the name and regiment, as seen on a marker for a veteran of the "colored infantry" (3.97). It was the family's responsibility to inscribe dates for birth and

Fig. 3.93. Concrete marker with brief inscription

Fig. 3.94. Concrete grave cover

death (3.98). It is not uncommon to find these markers used as replacement markers for memorializing the dead from the earlier Black Hawk, Mexican, and Spanish American wars (3.99, 3.100, 3.101). Government-issued Confederate markers (3.102) were made from marble with slightly pointed tops.[18]

It is suspected that many Civil War markers found in the western and northern portion of Illinois are the result of either veterans who moved to these areas after the war or veterans who were reburied by family members that relocated after the soldier's death.

Fig. 3.95. Early Civil War marker

Fig. 3.96. Later Civil War marker

Fig. 3.97. Civil War marker for member of U.S. Colored Infantry

Fig. 3.98. Civil War marker with added inscription for dates

Fig. 3.99. Civil War marker style, Black Hawk War

Fig. 3.100. Civil War marker style, Mexican War

Fig. 3.101. Civil War marker style, Spanish-American War

You can also expect to see a variety of metal plaques adjacent to stone grave markers (3.103). These were placed at the graves well after the initial burial by groups wanting to commemorate the veterans. The most common recognize veterans from the Revolutionary War, the War of 1812, and the Civil War.

Fig. 3.102. Civil War Confederate marker with pointed top

Fig. 3.103. Plaque to commemorate veteran

Looking Past the Grave

Family Plots

FENCES In Illinois, the Rural Cemetery movement began in the late 1850s (see chapter 4). One component of rural cemeteries was the use of family plots, which served the needs of the extended family. The number of burials in a family plot was, in part, determined by the family's status and wealth.

By the late 1800s it was common to see metal fences erected around family plots in a variety of different types of burial grounds (3.104). Fences were sold through local dealers, and a variety of styles could be chosen from catalogs. Chicago manufacturers provided many of the fences still seen in Illinois.

Some fence designs are quite intricate, and visitors should take the time to examine the different styles (3.105). One interesting style displayed in the Oak Hill Cemetery in Lewistown (Fulton County) is indicative of the rustic influence (3.106) discussed earlier.

Over time, the traditional fence design was modified, and masonry was combined with metal piping (3.107). As cemetery designs changed in the late 1800s, one of the goals was to create open vistas; thus, fences were prohibited. Eventually, many entire fences, and the rails used in later fences, were removed for scrap metal during World War I. The masonry corners may remain around the family plot (3.108).

Fig. 3.104. Iron fence

Fig. 3.105. Elaborate iron fence with anthropomorphic images

Fig. 3.106. Iron fence in the rustic design

Fig. 3.107. Family plot delineated with masonry and metal piping

Fig. 3.108. Family plot with masonry corners after piping had been removed

Fig. 3.109. Masonry family plot with stairs

Today, fences around family or individual plots are uncommon. Decay and the need for maintaining the grass has led to the dismantling of these once-prominent features. Although surviving catalogs provide images, it is still enjoyable to view the intricate designs up close.

COPING As noted above, family plots were first surrounded by fences. Eventually, the fences were replaced by low masonry boundaries called coping. The term is actually a misnomer since *coping* refers to the capstone atop masonry. Coping may have a small set of stairs to enter the family plot (3.109).

Fig. 3.110. Masonry coping in disrepair

Fig. 3.111. Partially buried coping

Coping can be found in many large rural cemeteries and in small Illinois cemeteries. Once its use was discouraged, however, the masonry fell into disrepair (3.110) and is now partially buried (3.111). As time goes by, more and more will disappear.

CORNER LETTERS In the early 1900s, as family plots were becoming less common, cemetery owners continued to restrict how the plots were marked. Fences and coping were no longer used; instead, family plots were marked with cornerstones, usually marble or granite. Each stone had the first initial of the family's last name inscribed on the top (3.112).

Fig. 3.112. Corner letters for family plot

Structures

RECEIVING VAULTS Digging graves into frozen ground was difficult. Many larger cemeteries used receiving vaults to store bodies until the graves could be excavated. These buildings were made from sandstone, marble, granite, brick, or concrete. They could be simple (3.113) or quite ornate (3.114), sometimes resembling mausoleums.

MAUSOLEUMS The late 1800s and early 1900s ushered in the use of mausoleums. A mausoleum is usually a building designed to house, above ground,

Fig. 3.113. Simple receiving vault

Fig. 3.114. More elaborate receiving vault

Fig. 3.115. Ornate mausoleum

Fig. 3.116. Less ornate mausoleum

Fig. 3.117. Earthen mausoleum

Fig. 3.118. Interior of Miles Mausoleum with compartments for caskets

one or more caskets. The building is usually elaborately designed (3.115), but simple mausoleums are also found in smaller cemeteries (3.116). Occasionally, a mausoleum was built as an earthen structure with a masonry entrance (3.117).

You can expect to see two types of mausoleums: nondynastic and dynastic.[19] Nondynastic mausoleums were built to house only the husband and, perhaps, his wife. Dynastic mausoleums house members of an extended family and may include husband, wife, children, their spouses, and grandchildren. An early dynastic mausoleum constructed atop the bluffs of the Mississippi River south of Columbia (Monroe County) was meant to hold over fifty bodies (3.118). It was built in 1858 at a cost of $28,000.

Mausoleums are clear expressions of wealth and status. Although rural and lawn cemeteries were meant to express equality among the dead (see chapter 4), the cost and appearance of these mausoleums expressed anything but equality. Mausoleums can be found in a variety of architectural styles including Egyptian, Greek, and Gothic. While marble and granite were common construction materials, brick and concrete were also used. Because these buildings came late in the development of rural cemeteries, they were usually found in close proximity to one another in newer portions of the cemetery. However, they can also be found taking advantage of terrain not otherwise suitable for burials (3.119). Two good examples of clustering can be found in Greenwood Cemetery in Decatur and Rosehill Cemetery in Chicago. When visiting Greenwood Cemetery, one gets the feeling of a small city of the dead, with roads leading to and around the structures (3.120). Marble and granite mausoleums often have ornate copper or bronze doors, stained-glass windows or door panels, and sculptures at the entrance.

In rural Illinois, it's not unusual to find an isolated mausoleum or, for that matter, a few mausoleums located throughout the cemetery. Sometimes the mausoleum is not elaborate but still gives the impression that some of the deceased were of higher status than others.

Some cemeteries have communal mausoleums that house the remains of individuals not related through blood or marriage (3.121). This practice became popular in the late 1800s and early 1900s. Today, the communal mausoleums located in small communities have created a financial burden as funding for maintenance and upkeep becomes scarce.

The use of mausoleums further reflects the ability to choose among a variety of options. In contrast, when pioneer burial grounds started, there were few options in how and where one was buried.

Vegetation

Along with grave makers and associated structures, burial grounds contain both native and nonnative vegetation. It is common to see flowers planted intentionally by a grave (3.122) or ornamental shrubs and trees growing adjacent to graves (3.123). You may also observe cedar trees used as a natural boundary around a burial ground (3.124). When burial grounds were first started, the first graves would likely not have been placed in areas encumbered by trees. Prairies or savannas, where trees were minimal, were probably the first locations chosen. Other open areas around farmsteads would also have been good options. The flowers found in the prairie would have provided a pleasant seasonal background to the graves (3.125).

Illinois has several pioneer burial grounds situated within prairies. Visitors

Fig. 3.119. Mausoleum on drainage slope

Fig. 3.120. Multiple mausoleums adjacent to roads

Fig. 3.121. Communal mausoleum

Fig. 3.122. Grave site with planted flowers

Fig. 3.123. Grave site with trees

Fig. 3.124. Trees along cemetery border

Fig. 3.125. Prairie flowers adjacent to grave site

Fig. 3.126. Mature tree within burial ground

to these sites have an opportunity to see both early grave markers and the remnants of the older prairies.

Many older burial grounds also provide an opportunity to see large trees that have not had their growth restricted by competition from other trees (3.126). The open space provided by these burial grounds enables the visitor to see older oaks and maples that might not appear elsewhere. Seeing these massive trees can greatly enhance the experience of visiting older burial grounds.

D. H. ARBOGAST
MAY 2, 1827
APR. 2, 1916
MINERVA PAYNE
HIS WIFE
MAY 28, 1829
APR. 1, 1914
ARBOGAST

CHAPTER 4
TYPES OF BURIAL GROUNDS

Burial grounds are places that have both sacred and secular meaning. Religious iconographic images, combined with written expressions of loss and eventual unification in heaven, are powerful expressions of sacred sentiment. In contrast, secular sentiments are represented by nonreligious folk art and written expressions of remembrance and love. For the living, the burial ground is a connection to the past. It contributes to a sense of community and reflects shared loss.

Despite the strong relationship between individuals and burial grounds, the broader communal relationship may weaken as family and friends move away. It is difficult to maintain a strong emotional association to a burial ground that contains strangers. These weakening bonds may eventually result in either neglect or abandonment, which then affects the appearance of the grounds. New burial grounds may be opened, with their own ties to the living. Despite inactivity and possible deterioration, however, abandoned burial grounds can inform us just as richly as active burial grounds.

All cemeteries are burial grounds, but not all burial grounds are cemeteries. The term *cemetery* did not come into use until the 1830s, when the Rural Cemetery movement began on the East Coast. Before then, the dead were placed in burial grounds (family- or community-based) or church graveyards. The word *cemetery* is derived from the Greek word *koimterian*, meaning "sleeping place."[1] As explained below in the section on rural cemeteries, the word was adopted as a way to alter our perceptions of death and memorialization. Thus, this relatively new term is more appropriately used to identify those burial places that share the characteristics of the rural cemetery and the later lawn cemetery. Its use is not appropriate for the early pioneer (family) burial grounds, church graveyards, or community burial grounds. However, it is common to find small rural burial grounds called cemeteries on entrance signs or even road signs.

Over time, the appearance of burial grounds has changed. In this chapter we examine the nine different types of burial grounds you are likely to encounter in Illinois. We discuss what factors caused burial grounds to evolve through the 1800s and 1900s and point out visual clues that will enable you to recognize these changes. The types of burial grounds include pioneer, church graveyard, community burial ground, rural cemetery, lawn cemetery, memorial park, military cemetery, battlefield burial ground, and institutional cemetery. Other terms are also used, such as *religious cemetery*, *family cemetery*, *municipal cemetery*, and *fraternal cemetery*; you may know of still more. These are variations of the types discussed below. However, even among the distinct types there are shared characteristics. Many marker types and landscape designs developed for a particular burial ground are seen in others as ideas and customs spread across the country.

Pioneer Burial Grounds

Traveling through central and southern Illinois in the early 1840s, William Oliver happened upon a burial ground. He describes a scene that would have been common in early 1800s Illinois.

> I was one day wandering through the woods in search of deer, when, in a lonely spot, overshadowed by some large oaks, I stumbled on five graves. There was no enclosure, nor anything to indicate the presence of a burial ground, beyond the unequivocal shape of mounds, and a few split rails arranged over each, to prevent an attack of the numerous bands of hogs. . . . I afterwards learned that this was the burying place of a family who lived on the borders of the prairies.[2]

(Note the reference to a burial ground rather than a cemetery.)

Pioneer burial grounds are the earliest historical burial places in Illinois. There are probably thousands of them. Many are abandoned and in need of attention. Because they contain the earliest burials, the pioneer burial ground is a wonderful place to see local, vernacular stone carvings that are sometimes highly stylized. They reflect a period of Illinois history when the population density was low and many folks lived on farms or in hamlets.

The earliest Euro-American settlements in Illinois were created by the French beginning in the late 1600s, primarily along the Illinois and Mississippi Rivers. To a lesser extent they also established settlements along the Wabash River in eastern Illinois. To our knowledge, French graves have never been identified in Illinois. These would have been simple graves. If they were marked, it would have been with wood or locally available rough stone.

In the early 1800s, Euro-American settlers ventured into the southern third of the state. These early settlers arrived from nearby southern states or came down the Ohio River from more eastern settlements. Therefore, southern Illinois is where some of the earliest documented burial grounds and markers may be found.

During the first third of the century, Illinoisans lived in a pioneer or frontier environment with scattered homesteads. Gradually, small settlements emerged along overland trails and adjacent to large streams as mills and ferries were established. Larger villages, towns, and cities with professional craftsmen and specialized merchants were yet to come. Consequently, some of the professional grave marker and burial ground traditions found in the eastern states were not yet present in Illinois. Death required burial on family homesteads or along transportation routes—that is, primitive trails and rivers.

Before churches were built, religious services and funerals took place in private homes and were attended by family and neighbors. In the absence of churchyards for burial, the pioneer burial ground represents one of the earliest types of sacred public place on the historical Illinois landscape. There would likely be a brief "public" religious ceremony at the grave site. In the absence of church buildings, grave markers with religious inscriptions or symbols are an early public expression of religious beliefs. Many early grave markers also contain folk art, making these burial grounds the earliest locations for displaying public art. As noted in chapter 3, professional stone carvers were scarce, but occasionally there is evidence for the work of these skilled craftsmen. Examples can be found in Oak Hill Cemetery in Lewistown (Fulton County) and Old Macomb Cemetery in Macomb (McDonough County).

Many of these small, early burial grounds are located on higher elevations near streams (4.1). These elevations provided grand vistas of the surrounding landscape. Higher ground may also have been chosen to avoid the threat of flooding. Where flooding was not an issue, lower elevations were sometimes used.

Pioneer burial grounds are also called family burial grounds because they began with a single burial but subsequently expanded as additional family members were buried. Over time, members of the extended family and sometimes neighbors were also buried in these grounds. Family clustering was common. Graves in pioneer burial grounds usually do not line up in neat rows but instead appear disorganized or random (4.2), in contrast with later cemeteries.

The graves of the first generation were frequently located on the highest ground, with later generations surrounding them (4.3). An *individual* marker

Fig. 4.1. Small burial ground atop hill

Fig. 4.2. Early markers not placed in straight rows

Fig. 4.3. Early grave markers in the foreground, later ones in the background

(as opposed to a group of markers) surrounded by later death dates indicates that the earlier marker was probably moved to that location. Conditions for moving markers from one burial ground to another are discussed later.

Walking through a pioneer burial ground, you will notice areas (usually in the middle) lacking markers but surrounded by other markers (4.4). The only evidence of graves may be either rectangular depressions or empty spaces. This is usually the location of the earliest graves. Grave depressions are particularly noticeable when the snow begins to melt; the snow covering the lower surface melts after the snow melts on the surrounding (more exposed) ground surface, creating low patches of snow. The absence of markers in these areas may result from deterioration of wooden markers, fallen and buried stones, graves that were never marked, or theft of markers.

Some people believe that because of their weight, many markers sink into the ground after they have fallen. In fact, the markers become covered as a result of earthworms bringing sediment up to the surface. In wooden areas, leaf litter also contributes to covering fallen markers (4.5).

Many pioneer burial grounds are found in the woods. It is highly unlikely the burials were originally placed in woods, as it would have been very difficult to dig graves through tree roots. Instead, the abandonment or neglect of pioneer burial grounds fostered the growth of trees and shrubs. The resulting woods create problems with access.

There are many reasons a pioneer burial ground may become abandoned or neglected. Current owners may be disinterested in those buried on their land when there is an absence of family ties. Even with family ties, the current generation may not carry a strong emotional bond with unknown family members from earlier generations. Finally, as society continues to distance itself from death, it develops a lack of concern for older burial grounds.

Churchyard Burial Grounds

Early settlers met in private homes for religious services. As more people settled in Illinois, formal church buildings were constructed. Many congregations also developed church graveyards for burying their dead (4.6). Unlike in the East, where there was a long history of established churches, Illinois churchyards did not get under way until the mid-1800s.

Over time, some churches were abandoned as new buildings were constructed in other locations, and some buildings were moved. In other instances, congregations may have disbanded or moved. Thus, many churchyard burial grounds are no longer associated with an active church. What may appear to be a community cemetery may actually be a churchyard minus the church. Absent signage about the former church, clues might be the presence

Fig. 4.4. Open areas void of markers but not of graves

Fig. 4.5. Partially buried marker

Fig. 4.6. Churchyard

of a large area void of any graves or the presence of large trees that may have once surrounded the building.

Community Burial Grounds

Early community burial grounds may have multiple origins, but a signature element is an emphasis on the burial of individuals who were not related through blood or marriage. The deceased likely shared residence in a small geographic area.

Many pioneer burial grounds transitioned into community burial grounds (4.7). Community burial grounds can be located within or adjacent to a town or city or out in the rural landscape (4.8). They developed in part to accommodate individuals who may not have owned land, such as those who lived or worked in town. A sentiment may also have developed among leading families to want their loved ones buried with others from the community.

Within community burial grounds that developed from pioneer burial grounds, one should expect to see a clustering of early death dates representative of the first family members. These early graves are usually clustered on higher elevations. Graves for nonfamily individuals will be found across the rest of the grounds.

Communities became more populated and widespread after the Civil War. Many burial grounds began to be built on the edge of towns. These did not evolve from the pioneer or family burial grounds. Families who had relatives buried in pioneer or family burial grounds frequently had the grave markers and remains of loved ones moved into these newer burial grounds. The motivation may have been a desire to have ancestors buried closer to where the family now lived, or the family may have simply been attracted to a "newer" burial ground and wanted to be part of it. The old pioneer burial grounds may have fallen into disrepair as burials ceased and family and friends moved further away. Within these community cemeteries, death dates prior to 1870 usually indicate markers that were moved.

Many of these cemeteries may also incorporate features common in rural cemeteries, such as internal roads, a few ornamental plantings, and family plots (discussed in greater detail later). Thus, although their size was small, the term *cemetery* is applicable.

Rural Cemeteries

Burial Grounds Become Cemeteries

Throughout Illinois are distinctive burial grounds characterized by rolling terrain, internal roads, family plots, elaborate and towering monuments, ma-

Fig. 4.7. Community burial ground in a rural setting

Fig. 4.8. Community burial ground in a town setting

ture trees and shrubs, and grand entranceways (4.9 and 4.10).[3] These are the signature characteristics of the rural cemetery. The Rural Cemetery movement began on the East Coast in response to a variety of factors prevalent in large cities. By the 1830s, these cities were besieged by rising poverty, disease, social inequality, and crime, creating a sense of despair for many inhabitants that cut across social and economic classes. Burial grounds in New York, Philadelphia, Boston, and Cambridge developed bad reputations due to deteriorating conditions caused by neglect and overcrowding. Civic leaders worried that conditions in the burial grounds contributed to community problems. Were

Fig. 4.9. Rural cemetery

Fig. 4.10. Rural cemetery entrance, Chicago

fumes from decaying bodies affecting the health of those who lived in close proximity? Were these burial grounds becoming a haven for crime because of their sense of abandonment? Burial grounds were located close to the city center, in sites viewed as good places for economic development. Thus, civic leaders embarked on what eventually became known as the Rural Cemetery movement.

Mount Auburn Cemetery in Cambridge, Massachusetts, created in 1830, was the first rural cemetery in the United States. The change in terminology from *burial ground* and *graveyard* to *cemetery* developed during this time. As mentioned before, *cemetery* comes from a Greek word denoting a sleeping room or dormitory. With that term came a fundamental shift in how we viewed death and the ways the dead would be memorialized. Loved ones were no longer viewed as dead but instead were thought to be resting or sleeping. By the late 1700s and early 1800s, there was a shift away from the earlier, more vivid images of death as represented by skulls and crossbones and toward more sentimental and reflective treatments. With the development of rural cemeteries, we see a multitude of symbols projecting loss and lives cut short along with epitaphs expressing strong emotions or sorrow. (See chapter 5 for a more detailed discussion on the iconographic images found on grave markers.)

The Changing Burial Landscape

At a time when citizens wanted to improve city life, the Rural Cemetery movement represents one aspect of change. The belief developed that living in close quarters among the dead may not be the best situation. The solution was to close the old, inner-city burial grounds, establish new places for the dead on the edge of the city, and move the burials from the old to the new grounds. These new burial grounds enhanced the well-being of city dwellers by creating a cultural landscape that, in addition to memorializing loved ones, could also be visited for visual and meditative pleasure (4.11). Essentially, there was now a place where the living and the dead could successfully coexist in a retreat from the rigors of city life. A related consequence was the availability of the old burial grounds within cities for future economic development.

The creation of rural cemeteries depended on a group of private citizens or an association to purchase land and employ a landscape architect to develop a site plan that brought together memorialization of the dead and elements of nature. After completion of internal developments including landscaping, roads, and perhaps an entrance gate, individual and family plots were sold.

The rural cemetery was designed as a final resting place where the dead could be memorialized without reflecting the social stratification characteristic of the living society. The notion that death was a state in which individuals might share a measure of equality was an important component of the movement. Family plots were encouraged; each plot would have a single marker representative of the family. In addition to moving the old city burial grounds, other smaller burial grounds and isolated burials from outside the city were moved to the new cemetery. Relocated burials help explain why rural cemeteries may contain older sandstone grave markers as well as marble markers with death dates older than the cemetery's founding.

In the past, burial grounds had been chosen for convenience and their natural setting. Graves were added close to family or friends. There would not be

Fig. 4.11. Rural cemetery with landscaped setting

any modification of the landscape other than the addition of the graves and perhaps a tree or flowers. In a rural cemetery, trees and shrubs, roads, family plots, and formal entrances were placed according to the goals of a designed landscape. Developers, wanting to make the cemetery part of nature, designed cultural landscapes based on formal English and French gardens.

The Rural Cemetery movement also incorporated an increasing interest in classical Greek and Egyptian architecture, as evidenced by the use of urns, pedestals, columns, and obelisks (see appendix C). As a result, the movement was an early venue for the development of American sculpture and public art, distinct from the folk art seen on earlier grave markers. Images now reflected a focus on loss, sentimentality, and remembrance (see chapter 5).

To enhance the goal of having the rural cemetery serve as a retreat from city life, printed guides were developed for the visiting public. These guides described and illustrated the cemeteries and encouraged the public to take advantage of their parklike settings.

Life insurance and membership in fraternal organizations also played an important role in cemetery development. In the beginning, life insurance was purchased specifically for the purpose of assisting the family with funeral expenses (4.12). In earlier times, when someone died, the family prepared the body for burial, dug the grave, transported the body, and made or paid for and erected the grave marker. Since others were now hired to perform these tasks, life insurance helped defray the costs. In addition, an individual or family plot needed to be purchased from the cemetery's owners. One benefit of membership in a fraternal organization was the ability to purchase a grave site in a section of the cemetery already set aside for the fraternal organization (4.13).

Fig. 4.12. Modern Woodmen Financial Planner

Fig. 4.13. Rural cemetery with a section for a fraternal organization

Family Plots

Family plots were an important feature that distinguished rural cemeteries from earlier burial grounds. Families were encouraged to purchase plots to accommodate members of the immediate family. The placement of these plots followed the cemetery design. The plots would be landscaped and managed by gardeners hired by the family.

Family plots were initially surrounded by iron fences. To soften the appearance, fences were eventually replaced by stone borders or coping. Once available, concrete coping became common. During the late 1800s and early

1900s, granite, and to a lesser extent marble, corner markers replaced fences and coping to designate family plots. Corner markers became common as cemetery owners tried to address the problems created by both fences and copings.

Creators of the concept of the rural cemetery were critical of what they saw as a society segregated by social and economic inequality. Organizers envisioned that at least in death, citizens could share some measure of equality. Thus, each family plot would have a single marker for the entire family. The intent was to achieve equality through similarity in markers. However, within the family plot inequality was still apparent, as husbands/fathers occupied a prominent place. Wives/mothers and children occupied a lower profile; their individual markers are frequently smaller and placement on the family marker is frequently below the husband/father's.

Illinois Rural Cemeteries Today

When visiting a rural cemetery, you will see success and failure. What began as an egalitarian treatment of family members through the use of a simple family marker quickly changed into expressions of status and wealth. Markers became larger and more ornate. Then, in addition to the family marker, individual markers of varying sizes and shapes for each family member were also erected.

Today, landscape elements such as trees and shrubs have grown and now obscure the view of interior markers. The result is that some rural cemeteries appear crowded, with little visibility into the cemetery (4.14).

In Illinois the earliest and most notable rural cemeteries appear in 1859 and 1860 in and around Chicago (Calvary, Rosehill, Graceland, Bohemian National, and Lake Forest). Other large cities, Rock Island (Chippiannock), Quincy (Woodland), Springfield (Oak Ridge), Decatur (Greenwood), and Peoria (Springdale) also developed cemeteries incorporating the defining features of a rural cemetery. The rural cemeteries in Chicago are noted for their well-designed landscapes and statuary art. Several are listed on the National Register of Historic Places (see chapter 7, table 7.4). These cemeteries include many of the features of the rural cemetery but on a smaller scale.

Communities in Illinois saw value in replicating all or some of the rural cemetery components, such as family plots, gates, and roads. By doing so, the people in Illinois chose to participate in a national movement that originated in the eastern states. Since the communities were smaller, either the components of the rural cemetery were modified and reduced in scale or fewer components were incorporated (4.15 and 4.16). Visitors can see local adaptations of the rural cemetery in small towns such as Barry and Pittsfield in Pike County and Highland in Madison County.

Fig. 4.14. Rural cemetery with crowded landscape and obscured view to interior

Fig. 4.15. Rural cemetery entrance, rural Sangamon County

Fig. 4.16. Rural cemetery entrance, rural Pike County

The cemeteries created through the Rural Cemetery movement reflect a coalescing of various social ideas and interests. In the end, the movement was a coming together of many different variables that collectively changed attitudes toward death and the way people memorialized the dead. In contrast to churchyard burial grounds, rural cemeteries helped create a secular approach to death and expanded the use of burial grounds as a forum for public art.

After several decades, the goals of the Rural Cemetery movement faltered, having achieved mixed results. Rural cemeteries were supposed to reflect parklike landscapes anchored by family plots and family markers. The status of the living would not necessarily be reflected in their markers. Instead, family plots often had central family monuments surrounded by individual markers of varying shapes and sizes, defeating the original goal of equality in death and often reflecting personal or family status and wealth. This trend culminated in the construction of nondynastic and dynastic mausoleums in the late 1800s (see chapter 3). In addition, the tranquility of open vistas was hampered by an abundance of trees and shrubs as well as by large markers placed adjacent to the roads (4.17). Metal fencing and masonry borders around family plots added to the clutter.

One of the goals of the Rural Cemetery movement had been that in death all would be treated equally. One's status in life would not be conveyed through elaborate family plots or markers. By the last quarter of the nineteenth century, however, family plots were starting to be used to display a family's status and wealth via heightened walls and entry steps, mimicking contemporary home

Fig. 4.17. Rural cemetery with large trees and large columns

Fig. 4.18. Family plot with masonry coping and stairs

Fig. 4.19. House with masonry coping and stairs

Fig. 4.20. Family plot identified as "our home"

Fig. 4.21. Lawn cemetery with small markers

designs. As seen in images 4.18 and 4.19, the family marker and home are both centered and surrounded by coping with entrance steps. In case there is still doubt, the next image (4.20) labels the family plot as "our home."

Lawn Cemeteries

In the 1850s, noted landscape architect Adolph Strauch transformed the Spring Grove Rural Cemetery in Cincinnati and introduced a new concept, the "lawn cemetery." Spring Grove had become overgrown and crowded. Strauch's new concept was more reflective of English gardens. The grounds were altered by thinning out vegetation and placing markers further back from the roads. Monuments were strictly regulated to a smaller and more uniform size, thus creating a greater sense of equality (4.21). Open vistas were created by the addition of ponds (not a common feature in Illinois lawn cemeteries). In today's Chicago's Rosehill and Graceland Cemeteries you will see a mix of design components from both rural and lawn cemeteries (4.22), in part because both concepts had already been introduced when the cemeteries were created.

With the introduction of lawn cemeteries, management of family plots was transferred from families to cemetery owners. Metal fences and masonry borders were prohibited and, in some cases, removed from around family plots. These changes achieved greater visual balance and also brought cemeteries closer to the goals first established by the Rural Cemetery movement.

Rural cemeteries reflected a great deal of sentimentality. Lawn cemeteries placed less emphasis on sentimentality by reducing the use of carved symbols and epitaphs. Lawn cemeteries also struggled to meet the goal of equality in

Fig. 4.22. Pond as a landscaping feature

Fig. 4.23. Memorial park with lawn plaque

Fig. 4.24. Memorial park with open view

Fig. 4.25. Memorial park sign

death. Monuments continued to vary in size, reflecting status and wealth. In addition, mausoleums became popular among those who could afford them.

Memorial Parks

As the concept of the lawn cemetery built on the goals of the Rural Cemetery movement, developers of the "memorial park" in the second decade of the 1900s expanded on the concepts that defined the lawn cemetery.[4] Memorial park owners further limited decision making for family and friends in several ways. First, marker style was restricted to a lawn plaque, placed flush to the ground, that recorded name, dates, and a few additional details (4.23). Second, the owners were responsible for lawn art and for maintaining open, reflective vistas (4.24). Third, the only grave decorations allowed were seasonal or temporary. Finally, the "cemetery" became a "park" (4.25).

In lawn cemeteries, displays of wealth and status were still a problem, as were crowding and a lack of open vistas, despite attempts to reduce marker size and clutter. In the new memorial parks, gone were the large columns and mausoleums. In the past, graves might have been marked with large statues that memorialized the dead. In memorial parks, statues were no longer placed at individual grave sites but were introduced as public art in the landscape design. Ponds, topographic relief, and vegetation also were incorporated into the landscape to create openness and tranquility. The term *park* evokes a more genteel and placid image and creates a certain distancing from the dead, in contrast to the word *cemetery*, which had become recognizable as a place to bury the dead. The new memorial park was designed as a place one might wish to visit or spend time, with less emphasis on the graves. Visitors first see the landscape rather than the markers.

While the appearance was cleaner and simpler, it also reflected changing consumer habits. Concepts that were "new" and "modern" appealed to a growing middle class willing to spend its money on a different approach to burial and memorialization. People had become disenchanted with grave markers that continued to reflect status and wealth. At the same time, there was increased interest in the development of urban parks. Just as the availability of marble, and later granite, provided an opportunity for nineteenth-century monument dealers and cemetery owners to market new products to consumers, the development of the memorial park also presented consumers with a new product. The use of uniform bronze markers minimized the role of monument companies and their suppliers; memorial park owners could now provide both marker and grave site.

The concept for a memorial park was initiated in Glendale, California, by Herbert Easton in 1913. In what is now known as Forest Lawn Memorial Park in Glendale, the visitor enters a place reflecting the Americans' desire to create greater distance between the living and the dead.

As burial places changed from "burial grounds" and "graveyards" to "rural" and "lawn" cemeteries, the deceased also changed from a state of "being dead" to "being asleep" or "at rest." With the memorial park concept, family and friends were now faced with fewer decisions. The use of a single style of a bronze marker placed flush with the ground produced uniformity of memorialization. Consequently, there were fewer expressions of personal grief and a lack of symbols expressing loss and death.

When you visit larger cemeteries, it is not uncommon to see characteristics of rural and lawn cemeteries intermixed with elements of memorial parks (4.26). Marble and granite are frequently erected side by side. Large obelisks or family plots are often adjacent to low granite markers. The ground-level plaques common to memorial parks may be in the same cemetery but are usually in separate areas away from the earlier markers. In some cemeteries you may be able to view all three cemetery types in close proximity to one another (4.27).

Military Cemeteries

National cemeteries were created in response to the high number of Civil War casualties. Burial of deceased soldiers from the Revolutionary War, the War of 1812, and the Mexican War was usually the responsibility of the family or fellow soldiers and took place in family burial grounds, in churchyards, or within battlefields. The number of deaths during the Civil War was unlike anything the country had ever experienced. The hundreds of thousands of dead and injured overwhelmed the public's ability to administer care to the injured while assisting in the burial of its dead. The federal government

Fig. 4.26. Rural and lawn cemeteries intermixed

Fig. 4.27. Addition of memorial park features to rural and lawn cemetery

eventually took responsibility for establishing national cemeteries to memorialize the war's dead, marking an important shift in responsibility from the family to the government. Specific locations were set aside to bury both the immediate battlefield dead (such as at Gettysburg) and those who died in POW camps and hospitals.[5]

The first national cemetery in Illinois was established at Mound City (Pulaski County) in 1864. Camp Butler, outside Springfield, was established soon after. In Alton (Madison County), the federal government maintains the Alton National Cemetery within the Alton Cemetery (4.28). In

Fig. 4.28. Federal military cemetery located within Alton Cemetery

Fig. 4.29. Military section within a rural cemetery

many large cemeteries such as Spring Hill in Danville (4.29), Woodland in Quincy, and Greenwood in Decatur, a section might be set aside for the burial and memorialization of dead soldiers. Civil War markers are typically arranged in rows or in a circle around a large statue of a soldier. The federal government is not responsible for care and maintenance of these sections. In Clinton (Dewitt County), the local city cemetery, Woodlawn, actually began as a burial place for the Civil War dead and evolved into a municipal cemetery.

Fig. 4.30. Confederate section within Camp Butler National Cemetery

In addition to Union war dead, Illinois also commemorates the burials of Confederate soldiers. In Alton a commemorative column marks the burial location of 1,354 Confederate POWs who died in the local camp due to illness. There are also sections for Confederate soldiers at Rock Island and Camp Butler in Springfield (4.30). Some individual burial grounds also have graves with markers designating Confederate dead.

Battlefield Burial Grounds

Illinois burial grounds contain many who have died during the nation's conflicts. As mentioned above, special sections or entire burial grounds have been set aside to honor veterans. However, you may be surprised to learn that Illinois actually has two battlefield burial grounds.

In 1832, during the Black Hawk War, the Illinois militia engaged Chief Black Hawk and his followers in two well-documented battles. The first was at Kellogg's Grove in western Stephenson County. Fighting lasted two days and resulted in the death of eight militia members. The dead were buried where they fell. Sometime later the graves were opened, and the dead were reinterred in a group burial east of the original graves. This location is now commemorated by a large obelisk. The graves are at the base, identified by individual markers. The markers are similar to the Civil War shield marker and no doubt were placed at a later date. Although they suffered their own causalities during the battle, we do not know where the fallen American Indians were buried.

A second battle occurred at Stillman's Run in Ogle County. Twelve militiamen were killed. Their marked graves are adjacent to a commemorative

Fig. 4.31. Stillman's Run Battlefield burial ground, Black Hawk War

monument erected in the 1890s. Similar Civil War–style markers were used here as well (4.31).

Institutional Burial Grounds

Several types of institutions had their own burial grounds, including poor farms, mental health facilities, orphanages, and homes for seniors. These were mostly active from the mid- to late 1800s, though several continued through the 1900s and even into the current century. What distinguishes these from the public and private burial grounds already discussed is the similarity of the grave markers, which frequently have a simple design. Those institutional burial grounds that span a long time may have headstones that show changes in style and design, but such changes usually occur after decades of using a single marker style. Frequently there is a shift in size or materials from stone to concrete. Institutional markers tend to be low to the ground with a plain design without motifs (4.32). No doubt these choices reduced cost. The markers are usually made of granite or concrete, or occasionally marble depending on the death dates. In many instances the grave marker may contain only the name and death date (the birth date may have been unknown), or even sometimes just a number (4.33). Once the institution closes, the burial ground is forgotten in the absence of family to maintain the grounds. The markers eventually become obscured by vegetation or are covered by later construction. Thus, many abandoned institutional burial grounds have fallen into disrepair or lie hidden under cultivated fields.

County poor farms frequently had their own burial grounds. When the facilities closed, the buildings were frequently razed. As a result, the only

Fig. 4.32. Institutional cemetery with similar marker shapes

Fig. 4.33. Institutional cemetery with numbered markers

aboveground reminders may be the grave makers from the burial ground. The Winnebago County Poor Farm outside Freeport is an example, where a few isolated markers serve as the only reminder of the old poor farm and its burial ground.

Large cemeteries may have a section containing burials from various institutions that did not have their own cemeteries. Such sections are noticeable at Woodland Cemetery in Quincy (4.34), Pontiac City Cemetery, Godfrey Cemetery in Jersey County, and Highland Cemetery in Madison County.

Fig. 4.34. Institutional section within a rural cemetery

If you see groups of markers in a large cemetery bearing similar or identical designs with limited information, they are most likely associated with institutional burials.

You may also see potter's fields (4.35 and 4.36) in some cemeteries. The Dodge Grove Cemetery (Coles County) still has a section identified for pauper burials. In contrast to other cemeteries, where the poor are buried along the cemetery's edge, Dodge Grove's pauper section is in a prominent location toward the middle of the cemetery.

Fig. 4.35. Potter's field

Fig. 4.36. Potter's field signage

To The
Memory of Mrs
of Jesse Benson
Who Departed
Aged 26 Y. 11 M.
& 25 D.

CHAPTER 5
GRAVE MARKER ICONOGRAPHY

Chapters 3 and 4 documented the different types of grave markers and burial grounds you should expect to see in Illinois. These differences are attributed in part to changing socioeconomic conditions, technological changes, and consumer choice. Another important feature of Illinois burial grounds is the iconographic images (folk art, religious images, mourning symbols, organization symbols, and other secular images) inscribed on grave markers. Several books and numerous websites explain a broad range of grave marker iconography;[1] it is unnecessary to repeat those efforts here. Instead, this chapter examines why these images were used and what factors caused them to change over time.

As scholars of grave markers have noted, historical iconographic images convey messages that may not be readily apparent today, hence the availability of resources meant to interpret these images. But why do these images even appear on grave markers? It has been suggested that during the seventeenth and eighteenth centuries, when illiteracy rates were high, symbols were a way to convey messages that could not otherwise be read.[2] However, in Illinois that is unlikely. Although illiteracy was probably high in the first half of the 1800s, it is more likely that the use of iconographic images was a continuation of tradition and was considered the norm. We are not aware of any markers with just images and no inscriptions.

In the eastern states, iconographic images have been used for over three hundred years. The popularity and decline of these images have been linked to broad social and religious factors.[3] In the Midwest, temporal trends are shorter and the iconographic images less diverse. Nevertheless, in Illinois changes are noticeable, and the reasons for those changes are similar to those associated with changes in both grave markers and burial grounds.

The Early 1800s

In the early 1800s, most Illinois grave markers included only the deceased's name accompanied by birth date, death date, or both. Less frequently, markers might contain iconographic images. Sandstone was the predominant material at the time. When visiting burial grounds, it is always worthwhile to look at these markers to see if any contain these distinct images. These carvings required the skill of a professional carver, which would have been costly; we have not seen "homemade" markers with images. This higher cost may have affected the frequency with which images were used.

These early images fall into two categories, secular folk art and religious symbolism. We should remember that in the early 1800s, Illinois had few public buildings. Hence, in contrast to the eastern states, there was an absence of public places to display art. Examples of art were more commonly incorporated into households through pictures, tableware, furniture, and house designs. One of the few public places for displaying art was in the burial ground.

Within the eastern states, designs found on mirrors, bed frames, dressers, and door frames are sometimes also found on grave markers (5.1 and 5.2). However, displays in one's home were mostly private. When applied to the grave marker, these images became an expression of public art, a tradition that continues today. Designs on early grave markers conformed to types previously known, and their artistic expressions were appreciated and accepted by the community.

Because many eastern carvers signed their markers, researchers are able to study the quality and geographic extent of their work. In Illinois, few early carvers signed their work. We are not aware of any published studies documenting the early work of Illinois grave-marker carvers or assessing folk art on grave markers in Illinois. Geometric designs (5.3), vegetation (5.4), and anthropomorphic (5.5) representations are types of secular folk art seen in Illinois.

In the northeastern colonial states, the changes in images carved on grave markers represent, in part, altering attitudes toward death and a willingness to incorporate religious symbols. The earlier markers reflected a Puritan view, which prohibited religious symbols and saw life as short and death inevitable.[4] There was a lack of sentimentality for what awaited all of us. Death heads, skeletons, scythes, and other harsh images were common. Over time, this Puritan view was replaced by one that expressed more sentiment and emotion. The prohibition against religious symbols was also dropped. The

Fig. 5.1. Common design on 1800s door frames

Fig. 5.2. Common design on 1800s mirrors and bed frames

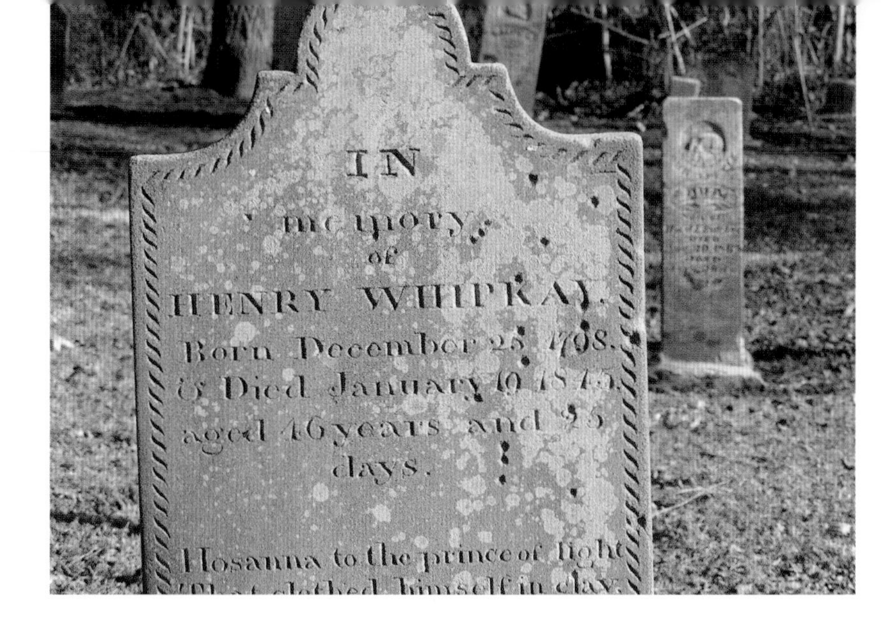

Fig. 5.3. Secular art—geometric design

Fig. 5.4. Secular art—vegetation

Fig. 5.5. Secular art—human-like face

Fig. 5.6. Early image of a flying cherub

Fig. 5.7. Flying cherub on marble

transition toward sentimentality is demonstrated by death heads evolving into flying cherubs (5.6). Two other common transitional images, the urn and the willow tree, expressed a more meditative reflection on death and an awareness of the opportunity for eternal life.[5]

As noted in chapter 3, in Illinois the earliest image we have seen that reflects on death is the flying cherub, dated 1837, in the Vermilionville Cemetery in northern Illinois. The sandstone marker memorializes Deacon John T. Ross. Although carved much later, we have also seen a flying cherub on a marble marker (5.7). This is an example of the continuation of an image from an

Fig. 5.8. Early image of an urn

Fig. 5.9. Early image of a willow tree

Fig. 5.10. Use of urn and willow tree together

Fig. 5.11. Catherine Ayres grave marker, with multiple images

Fig. 5.12. Detail of C. Ayres marker; note the grave marker beneath the willow tree

Fig. 5.13. Detail of C. Ayres marker; note the second grave marker beneath a budding flower

earlier time, even after more "modern" symbols associated with the Victorian period (see below) became more prevalent. The urn and willow tree were the more commonly used religious images during this period (5.8 and 5.9). Each is a symbolic contemplation on loss and renewal. The urn may occur by itself or combined with a tree (5.10).

One unusual marker carved by an unknown craftsman is the Catherine Ayres marker in the Hillsboro Cemetery. The loss felt at her death in 1844 at the age of twenty-two is symbolized by a centrally placed willow tree and a lamb off to the side (5.11). Both images are Christian expressions of mourning, with the lamb possibly reflecting her young age. Especially noteworthy is the inclusion of two images of grave markers, one partially hidden under the willow tree (5.12) and a more noticeable one under a nearby flower (5.13). Close examination of this image shows an attempt to illustrate inscriptions on the image of the marker.

The Mid-1800s

By the mid-1800s, Illinois grave markers and burial grounds had undergone significant changes. Along with the introduction of rural cemeteries and their local variants, there was also a shift in the types of iconographic images used on markers. The most significant change was the adoption of themes associated with what is now referred to as the Victorian Period of Death. Over the course of forty years, England's Queen Victoria mourned the death of her husband, Prince Albert. During this time, funeral rituals, public displays of mourning, special clothing, and grave-marker designs reflected, in part, a strong sense of personal loss softened by knowledge that a loved one was now comforted by Jesus.[6]

With the arrival of marble and the rise of commercial monument dealers, the use of sandstone markers diminished. The folk art present on many sandstone markers was replaced on marble markers by iconographic images symbolizing loss and salvation. In cemeteries throughout Ohio, Indiana, and Illinois, you will see the same images repeated on marble markers. Consumers now had the opportunity to choose images from a catalog, and these iconographic images were treated like other consumer products: they were mass-produced and widely available. Monument dealers found a public ready to be identified with the modern values expressed by these products (5.14, 5.15).

Nonreligious themes also represented on marble markers included patriotism (5.16 and 5.17) and membership in fraternal organizations such as Masons (5.18), Odd Fellows, or Woodmen of the World. The use of these images was almost exclusively restricted to males. Most of the patriotic images probably reflect service during the Civil War. Many secular organizations

Fig. 5.14. Marble markers were popular for their time

Fig. 5.15. Example of a marker image available from a catalog

Fig. 5.16. Patriotic theme

Fig. 5.17. Military theme and courage

Fig. 5.18. Mason symbol

provided members assistance in covering the costs for funerals and burial. In addition, membership brought status to the individual. Recognition of these factors was frequently conveyed by including the organization's symbol on the grave marker.

The Late 1800s and Early 1900s

By the late 1800s, grave markers had changed. Marble columns became more prevalent, and zinc and sculptured limestone were introduced. Along with these new marker types came a move away from the romanticized images associated with the Victorian Period of Death. The mournful images common on tablet markers are not commonly found on columns; exceptions include clasped hands (5.19) and vegetation (5.20). On many cross-vault columns (see appendix C), images of gates and the kingdom of heaven are more common (5.21).

As noted in chapter 3, the rustic style, with an emphasis on plants and natural images (5.22), is closely associated with limestone sculptures. These images are, in part, a rejection of the mournful themes common to the earlier marble markers. It is difficult to classify these rustic images as folk art since many were replicated from images presented in catalogs and may not have been locally produced.

Occasionally, religious themes are applied to limestone markers in conjunction with rustic images (5.23). The use of crosses is usually a Catholic

Fig. 5.19. Clasped hands

Fig. 5.20. Vegetation on a cross-vault column

Fig. 5.21. Heavenly gates carved on a cross-vault column

Fig. 5.22. Tree trunk with personalized art

Fig. 5.23. Religious and secular-themed tree trunk grave marker

Fig. 5.24. Personalized plaque for a zinc marker

Fig. 5.25. Grave marker imagery changed with the use of granite

rather than a Protestant practice. In these instances, crosses were added to what was probably a secular marker selected from a catalog.

Zinc markers were marketed by salesmen, and consumers made selections from catalogs. Because these markers were hollow and included decorative insert panels, the iconographic images could be changed or combined as the consumer wished (5.24). There was an emphasis on decorative designs rather than symbols denoting mourning, loss, and salvation.

The late 1800s saw the introduction of granite grave markers, and this material quickly became the choice of consumers, perhaps for its durability and

Fig. 5.26. Modern Woodmen of America symbol

Fig. 5.27. Religious symbolism common throughout history

Fig. 5.28. Personal photographs common among ethnic groups

Fig. 5.29. Laser technology used to personalize granite marker

Fig. 5.30. Early image on a granite replacement marker

color options. Concurrent with this change in material came a reemphasis on democratizing the cemetery by standardizing marker size and shape. As a result, the iconographic images focusing on mourning, loss, and salvation disappeared. Instead, images were almost exclusively restricted to decorative designs (5.25), again obtained through catalogs. Symbols for secular organizations continued (5.26), as did the use of religious symbols (5.27).

Another change in the late 1800s was the introduction of photographs. In Illinois, this practice was prominent among certain ethnic groups. The Norway Cemetery south of Norway (5.28) and the Russian Orthodox Cemetery near Benld are two places where markers, both marble and granite, include photographs. In the late 1900s, photographs and laser-engraved replicas gained popularity. Lasers provide opportunities to engrave additional secular images such as aerial views of farms (5.29) and illustrations showing the deceased engaged in favorite pastimes. By the late 1900s, on replacement markers there was a revival of images common in the early 1800s, such as the willow tree (5.30).

CHAPTER 6
VISITING BURIAL GROUNDS

All burial grounds have something interesting to see. Whether you are interested in folk art from the early 1800s carved into sandstone markers, want to study the landscapes and sculptures of the late 1800s rural cemeteries in Chicago, or simply enjoy the excitement of walking through any type of burial ground, Illinois has a wide assortment of places to visit. To help you find what you may be looking for, chapter 7 presents a representation of all the types of burial grounds, markers, and iconographic images found in Illinois. In addition to the burial grounds listed in the next chapter, we hope you are encouraged to venture out and find new places to visit.

Locating a Burial Ground

We provide a few guidelines to help locate grounds you have not yet visited. Several sources can be helpful, including county histories, county road maps, newspaper obituaries, and online resources (see below). Sometimes one source will point you in the direction of another source. You can occasionally learn about burial grounds from unusual sources such as personal letters, family diaries, and postcards. Finally, you can verify the location of the burial ground by taking a drive and examining the landscape for visible clues. Some clues can be obvious, such as a road name, a cemetery sign, or grave markers. Other clues may be more subtle, like an isolated clump of trees in a field (6.1). Look closer and you may see grave markers (6.2).

There are several good places to begin your search. Start with historical documents at the library and local and state historical and genealogical societies. They have county histories, historical atlases and plat maps (6.3), and

Fig. 6.1. Nearly hidden grave marker in the woods

Fig. 6.2. Close-up showing the single grave marker in the woods

even cemetery books. Some counties have mapped many burial grounds and have made the information available. Many genealogical and historical societies also have web pages to assist the long-distance researcher.

When driving, watch for road signs that clearly indicate a burial ground nearby (6.4). Sometimes a cemetery will have multiple names (6.5), but only one of those names may be used in the historical documents. You can also consult USGS topographic maps (6.6) and historical aerial photographs to confirm a possible location. Sometimes a county highway map will show

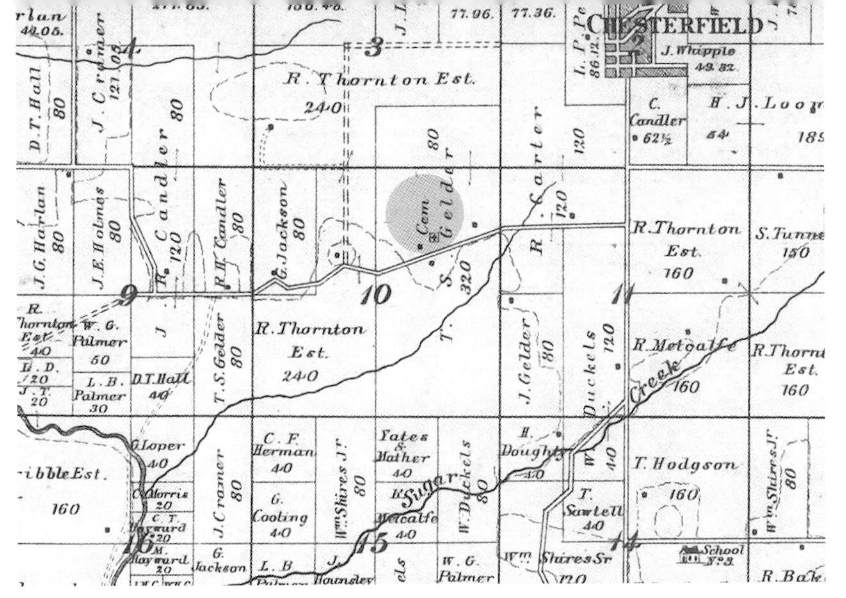

Fig. 6.3. Burial ground noted on a historic atlas map. Reproduced from Warner and Beers, 1875, *Atlas Map of Macoupin Co. and the State of Illinois*, Chicago.

Fig. 6.4. Road sign indicating a nearby burial ground

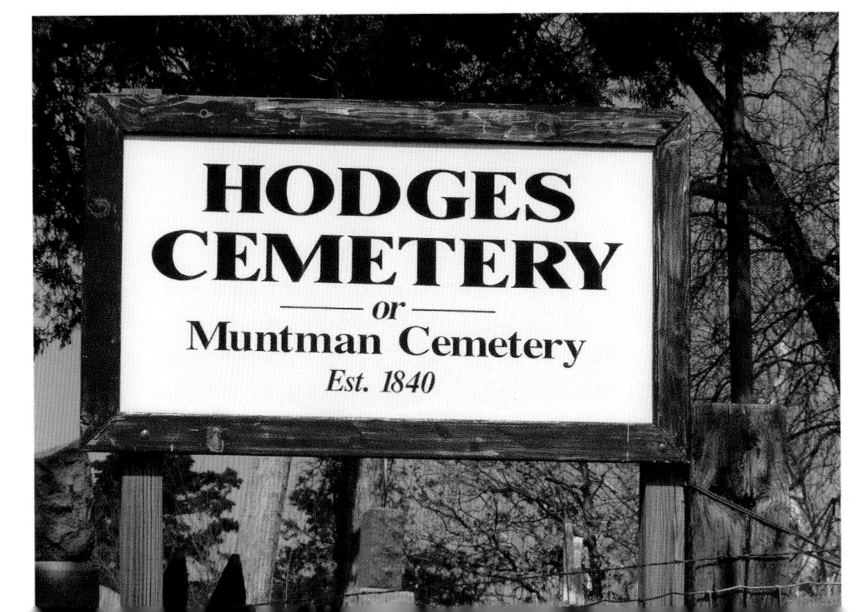

Fig. 6.5. Burial ground with multiple names

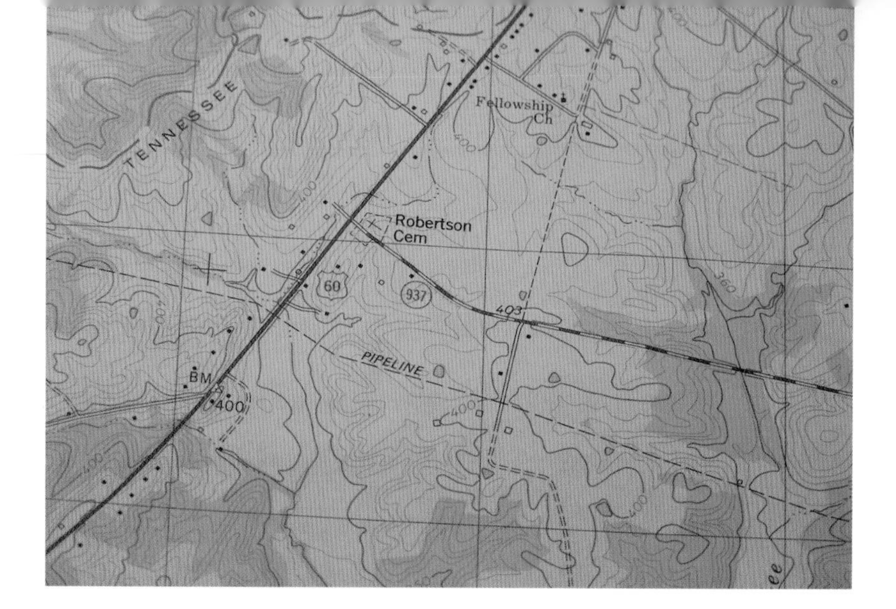

Fig. 6.6. Location of a cemetery on a USGS topographic map

cemetery locations. Many of these sources are available at your local university library and the Illinois State Library in Springfield.

If the cemetery has a sexton or is managed by a board, they might have a plat of the cemetery. A plat shows the layout of the grave plots and may also show roads and streams.

Often the best sources of information are people from nearby communities. You never know unless you ask, "Have you ever heard of the old Shipman Cemetery?" We have found that one of the best times to visit a cemetery is the weekend before Memorial Day because people will be preparing the grounds and grave markers for the holiday. These people tend to be knowledgeable about the cemetery and can be very helpful.

Once you find a burial ground, take time to explore the area before you begin to take photographs. People tend to focus on the markers and do not see the whole picture. Also, by getting acquainted with the grounds, you will note areas that may have hidden markers (6.7). Remember that if you do not see anything of interest as you drive by, it might be because earlier markers have fallen over (6.8). We have frequently debated about getting out of the car and exploring what appears to be a sea of sameness. The decision to venture out is rewarded when an unexpected early sandstone marker is discovered.

Pay attention to your safety. Tell someone where you will be going, and pack the right equipment.

Equipment

The following items are useful to have with you when visiting a burial ground. Sturdy shoes are essential. Sandals and other open-toed shoes can lead to injury if you trip on a partially buried marker or a tree root. It's always good to

Fig. 6.7. Overgrown vegetation obscures grave marker

Fig. 6.8. Fallen grave markers

pack rain gear for unexpected rain showers. Remember to dress appropriately for the weather. Some markers are best observed in winter, so take precautions for cold weather, especially against the biting winds blowing across the landscape. In contrast, warm weather presents its own challenges—intense sun and heat, biting insects, and poison ivy. A hat, extra water, sunscreen, and insect repellent are must-have items in your tool kit. A cell phone and charger are vital in an emergency.

Additional items to include in your kit are road maps (some will show cemetery locations), digital camera with extra batteries, flashlight, notebook,

Fig. 6.9. Death date nearly illegible

Fig. 6.10. Death date illuminated with the aid of a flashlight

and pen. The flashlight can be used to highlight the inscription on a worn marker (6.9): if you shine the light across the inscription from the side to create a shadow, what you are trying to read should be made more visible (6.10). You can also use a mirror to reflect light onto a worn marker. A notebook is handy when you want to record any unusual features or notes about the cemetery. Mark the cemetery's location on a road map so you can visit again or tell others how to find it. The digital camera and extra batteries are obvious choices if you'd like to take photographs; you'd be surprised how many people forget to take them. Finally, have snacks and water with you. In the excitement of discovery, you might forget to eat or drink. Always remember to keep hydrated, even during the winter months.

Etiquette

Burial grounds are both public and private spaces and serve as a "final resting place." Visitors should follow proper etiquette. Follow posted cemetery rules, such as hours of operation, placement of flowers, and speed limits. Be mindful of where you drive and park your vehicle, always staying on paved or graveled roadways. Driving or parking on soft ground can cause ruts.

Never pick up or move a grave marker. If a marker is turned upside down and you are unable to read it, avoid the temptation to turn it over; doing so may cause the marker to break. Instead, check with the local historical or genealogical society, as the burial ground may already be documented and the information otherwise available.

Visitors are expected and encouraged. If you come upon a gate that is closed but not locked, it is okay to enter. You should never climb over a locked gate. Be sure to close all gates when you leave. Landowner permission may be required to access a burial ground that is entered from a private lane.

Remember, burial grounds have much to offer, and by following proper etiquette, you will ensure that others will be able to enjoy a similar experience.

CHAPTER 7
PLACES TO VISIT

This chapter includes three maps that divide the state into sections, North, Central, and South, identifying burial grounds to visit. Thus, if you are limited in your travel, you will still have an opportunity to visit an assortment of interesting burial grounds. The numbers on the map are keyed to the names of the burial grounds listed in the accompanying tables. Each table identifies specific characteristics of the burial grounds. For example, Woodland Cemetery is labeled 36 and appears on the Central map. The table codes Woodland Cemetery as R (rural cemetery), SS (early sandstone markers), and Z (zinc). At the end is a table for all the burial grounds in Illinois that are listed on the National Register of Historic Places. We have tried to include the nearest town for each burial ground.

Burial grounds and cemetery locations can be found at the following online resources:

- Find a Grave (http://www.findagrave.com/) can help you locate cemeteries and some individual graves; may include map location, list of burials, and some photographs of cemetery and/or individual graves.
- Genealogy Trails (http://www.genealogytrails.com/) is a source for cemeteries, genealogy, and history by state and county.
- Graveyards of Illinois (http://www.graveyards.com/) lists cemeteries alphabetically by county; cemetery location and map are provided when known; photographs mainly show entrances or general views of the cemeteries.

- Illinois Ancestors: Your Path into the Past (http://www.illinoisancestors.org/) is a history and genealogy website for twenty Illinois counties; it contains information on cemetery locations and markers transcriptions listed by cemetery.

Some local libraries and genealogical and historical societies have digitized cemetery books, historical plat maps and atlases, and county histories. Another method for locating specific burial grounds is simply to use a search engine, putting the cemetery name, county name, and state in your search.

Table 7.1. North

#	Cemetery Name	Town, County	Features of Interest
1	Kellogg's Grove	Near Kent, Stevenson Co.	B
2	Stillman's Run	Stillman Valley, Ogle Co.	B
3	Rosehill	Chicago, Cook Co.	R
4	Graceland	Chicago, Cook Co.	R
5	Bohemian National	Chicago, Cook Co.	R, LS
6	St. James Catholic Church	Lemont, Cook Co.	NR
7	Chippiannock	Rock Island, Rock Island Co.	NR, R
8	National Cemetery	Rock Island Arsenal, Rock Island Co.	M
9	Confederate Cemetery	Rock Island Arsenal, Rock Island Co.	M
10	Colony Cemetery site	Bishop Hill, Henry Co.	E
11	Munson Township	South of Geneseo, Henry Co.	P
12	Oakwood	Geneseo, Henry Co.	R
13	Oakland	Princeton, Bureau Co.	Z
14	Vermilionville	Vermilionville, La Salle Co.	SS
15	Norway	Norway, La Salle Co.	E
16	Elmwood	Yorkville, Kendall Co.	R
17	Hope	Galesburg, Knox Co.	R, ML
18	Babb	East of Lacon, Marshall Co.	SS
19	Hall	East of Lacon, Marshall Co.	SS
20	St. Mary	East of Lacon, Marshall Co.	SS
21	Mound Grove	Kankakee, Kankakee Co.	R, V

Key

B = Battleground
E = Ethnic
LS = Limestone
M = Memorial Park
ML = Mausoleum
NR = National Register
P = Pioneer
R = Rural
SS = Sandstone
V = Vegetation
Z = Zinc

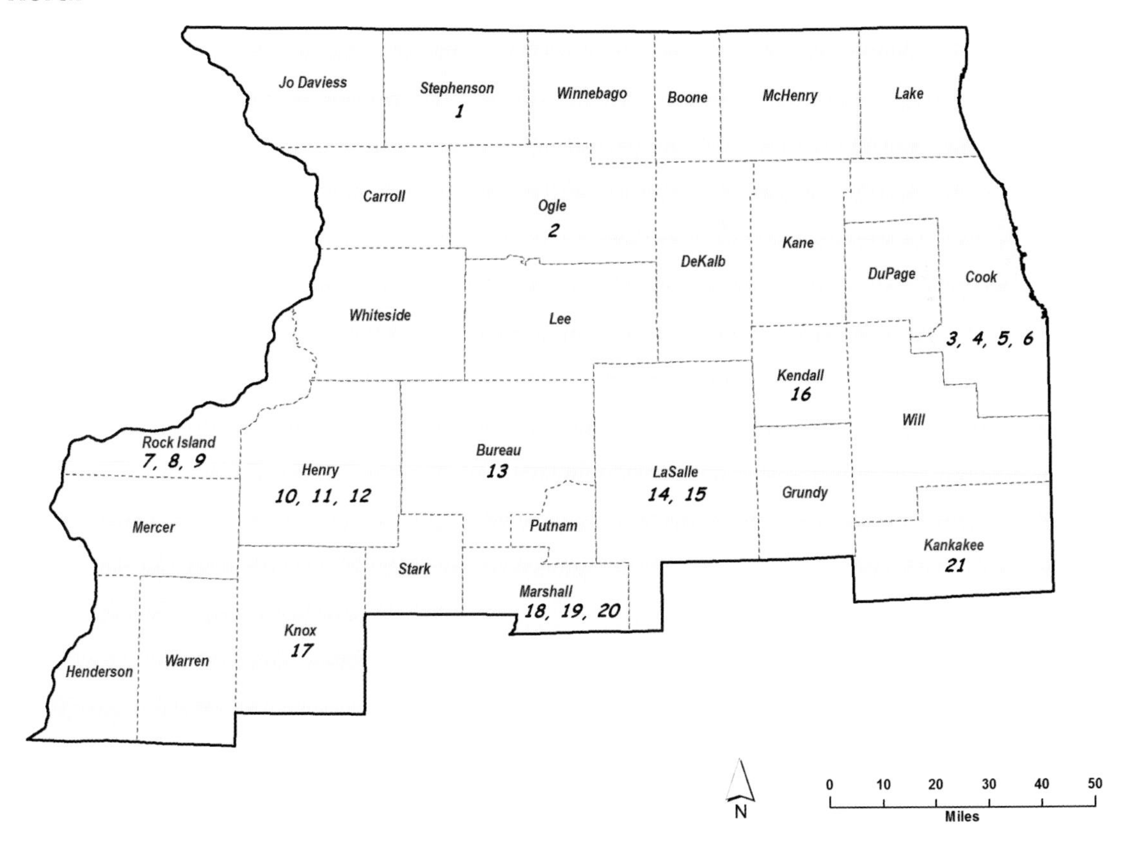

North
Jo Daviess
Stephenson
1
Winnebago
Boone
McHenry
Lake
Carroll
Ogle
2
DeKalb
Kane
DuPage
Cook
Whiteside
Lee
3, 4, 5, 6
Kendall
16
Will
Rock Island
7, 8, 9
Henry
10, 11, 12
Bureau
13
LaSalle
14, 15
Grundy
Mercer
Putnam
Kankakee
21
Stark
Marshall
18, 19, 20
Knox
17
Henderson
Warren
N
0
10
20
30
40
50
Miles

Map 7.1. North

Table 7.2. Central

#	Cemetery Name	Town, County	Features of Interest
22	Augusta	Augusta, Hancock Co.	Z
23	Old Nauvoo	Nauvoo, Hancock Co.	SS
24	Atkinson-McCord	Colchester, McDonough Co.	P
25	Old Macomb	Macomb, McDonough Co.	SS
26	Bean	East of Colchester, McDonough Co.	P, SS, V
27	Oak Hill	Lewistown, Fulton Co.	R, M, L, SS
28	Springdale	Peoria, Peoria Co.	P
29	Dickison	Peoria, Peoria Co.	C; variety of markers
30	Roanoke	Roanoke, Woodford Co.	L
31	Winkler	Germantown Hills, Woodford Co.	cherubs
32	Pontiac City	Pontiac, Livingston Co.	R, Z
33	Oak Hill	Watseka, Iroquois Co.	R, LS, CW
34	Evergreen	Bloomington, McLean Co.	R
35	Oak Grove	Leroy, McLean Co.	R, SS, "relic"
36	Woodland	Quincy, Adams Co.	R, SS, Z
37	St. Peter's	Quincy, Adams Co.	E, R
38	Walker and William	East of Liberty, Adams Co.	SS
39	Beardstown City	Beardstown, Cass Co.	R, SS
40	Woodlawn	Clinton, DeWitt Co.	CW, R
41	Cundiff	Weldon Springs State Park, DeWitt Co.	P
42	Blue River	South of Detroit, Pike Co.	SS
43	Barry	Barry, Pike Co.	R, L, M
44	Naples	Naples, Scott Co.	R, SS
45	Jacksonville East	Jacksonville, Morgan Co.	R, SS
46	Constant	Southeast of Buffalo Hart, Sangamon Co.	LS
47	Fancy Creek	North of Sherman, Sangamon Co.	R, SS
48	Oak Ridge	Springfield, Sangamon Co.	R; Lincoln's tomb
49	Old Stonington	Southeast of Stonington, Christian Co.	R
50	Rosemond Grove	Southeast of Rosamond, Christian Co.	R
51	Greenwood	Decatur, Macon Co.	R, FP, ML
52	Oak Grove	Jerseyville, Jersey Co.	R, CW, SS, LS
53	Carlinville	Carlinville, Macoupin Co.	R, "former slave"
54	Russian Orthodox	Near Benld, Macoupin Co.	E
55	Oak Grove	Hillsboro, Montgomery Co.	SS
56	Livingston	East of Marshall, Clark Co.	O

Key

C = Community	LS = Limestone	R = Rural
CW = Civil War	M = Memorial Park	SS = Sandstone
E = Ethnic	ML = Mausoleum	V = Vegetation
FP = Family Plot	O = Ovoid	Z = Zinc
L = Lawn	P = Pioneer	

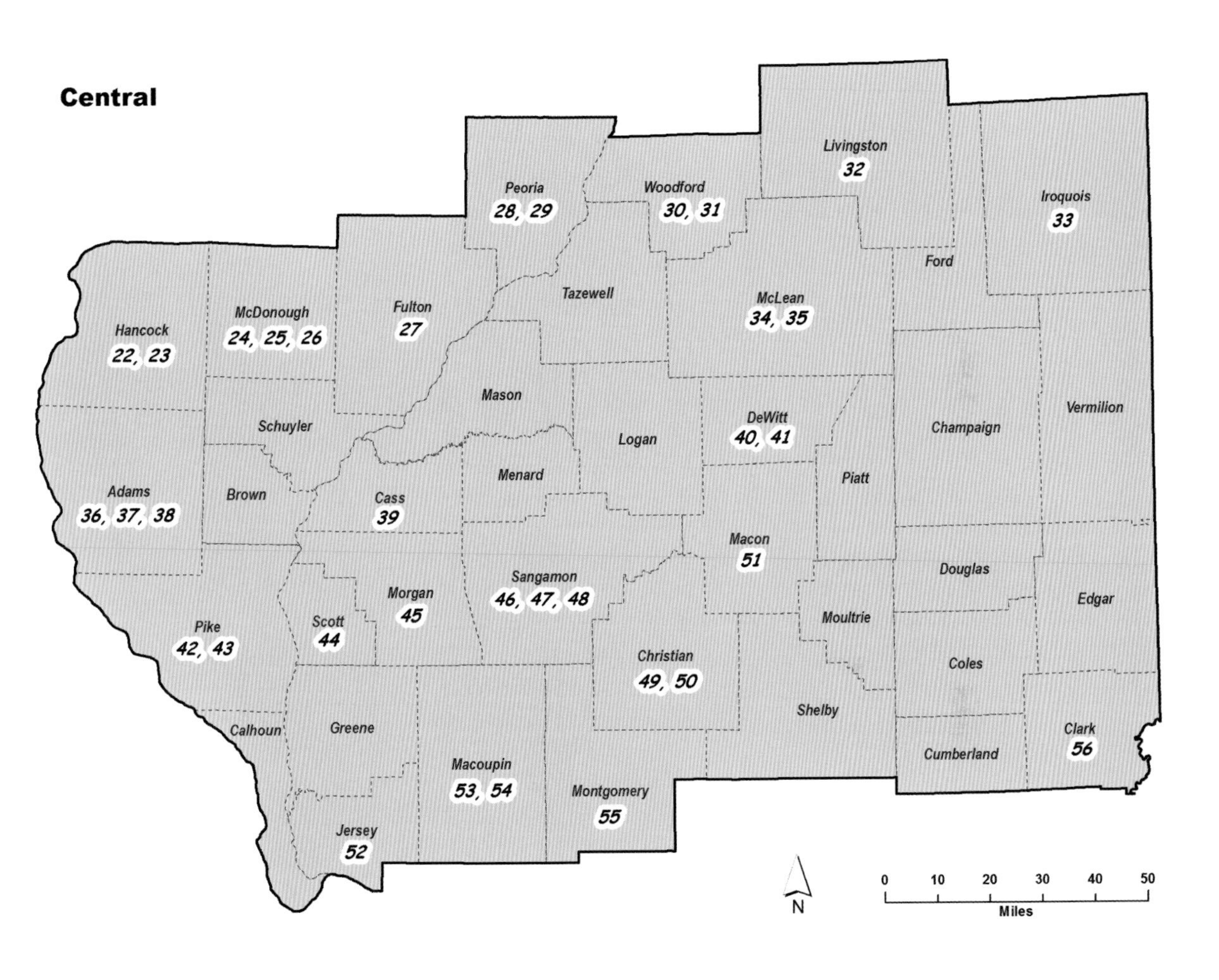

Map 7.2. Central

Table 7.3 South

#	Cemetery Name	Town, County	Features of Interest
57	Godfrey	Godfrey, Madison Co.	R, I
58	Highland	Highland, Madison Co.	R, E
59	Old State	Vandalia, Fayette Co.	SS, statehouse
60	Newlin	North of Robinson, Crawford Co.	SS
61	Sand Hill	Mt. Carmel, Wabash Co.	early slate
62	Palmier	Columbia, Monroe Co.	SS
63	Miles (Eagle Cliff)	North of Valmeyer, Monroe Co.	SS, ML
64	Dennis Hollow	Valmeyer, Monroe Co.	SS
65	Deer Hill	West of Waterloo, Monroe Co.	E
66	Evangelical St. Marcus	North of Red Bud, Monroe Co.	SS, folk art
67	Hopewell	West of Pinckneyville, Perry Co.	SS, V
68	Old Graveyard	Carmi, White Co.	SS, box tombs
69	Woodlawn	Carbondale, Jackson Co.	R
70	Hogan	Southwest of Shawneetown, Gallatin Co.	SS
71	Equality Village	Equality, Gallatin Co.	SS, box tombs

Key

E = Ethnic
I = Institutional
ML = Mausoleum
R = Rural
SS = Sandstone
V = Vegetation

South
Effingham
Fayette
59
Jasper
Crawford
60
Bond
Madison
57, 58
Clay
Richland
Lawrence
Clinton
Marion
Saint Clair
Wayne
Edwards
Wabash
61
Washington
Jefferson
Monroe
62, 63, 64, 65
Randolph
66
Perry
67
Hamilton
White
68
Franklin
Jackson
69
Williamson
Saline
Gallatin
70, 71
Hardin
Union
Johnson
Pope
Alexander
Pulaski
Massac
N
0
10
20
30
40
50
Miles

Map 7.3. South

Table 7.4. Illinois burial grounds listed on the National Register of Historic Places

Burial Ground	City	County
Alton National*	Alton	Madison
Benjamin Friends Meeting House and Burial Ground	Holder	McLean
Bohemian National	Chicago	Cook
Camp Butler*	Springfield	Sangamon
Chippiannock	Rock Island	Rock Island
Danville National*	Danville	Vermilion
Ebenezer Methodist Episcopal Church and Cemetery	Golden	Adams
Free Frank McWorter grave site	Barry	Pike
Graceland	Chicago	Cook
Lake Forest	Lake Forest	Lake
Mound City*	Mound City	Pulaski
Oak Hill	Lewistown	Fulton
Oak Ridge	Springfield	Sangamon
Quincy National*	Quincy	Adams
Rock Island National*	Moline	Rock Island
South Henderson Church and Cemetery	Gladstone	Henderson
Springdale	Peoria	Peoria
St. James Catholic Church and Cemetery	Lemont	Cook
Union Miners	Mt. Olive	Macoupin
Woodland	Quincy	Adams
Woodlawn	Carbondale	Jackson

*national cemeteries

In addition, three Confederate cemeteries are located in Illinois:

- Confederate Mound in Oak Woods Cemetery, Chicago, Cook County (National Register nomination in progress)
- North Alton Confederate Cemetery, Alton, Madison County (National Register nomination in progress)
- Rock Island Confederate Cemetery, Rock Island, Rock Island County

PHEBE.

APPENDIX A
PREHISTORIC MOUNDS TO VISIT

The listed mounds are open to the public unless otherwise noted.

Prehistoric Mounds

A Dunleith Mounds, Gramercy Park, East Dubuque, Jo Daviess County
B John Chapman Archaeological Site and Wapello Land and Water Reserve, south of Hanover, Jo Daviess County
C Albany Mounds, east side of Albany, Whiteside County
D Sinnissippi Mounds, Sinnissippi Park, Sterling, Whiteside County
E Beattie Park Mounds, Beattie Park, Rockford, Winnebago County
F Briscoe Mounds, southeast of Channahon, Will County
G Indian Mounds Park, Fifth & Harrison Streets, and Parker Heights Park, North Bottom Road; both in Quincy, Adams County
H Dickson Mounds State Park and Ogden-Fettie Mound, east of Lewistown, Fulton County
I Pere Marquette State Park, Illinois Route 100, west of Grafton, Jersey County
J Cahokia Mounds State Historic Site, west of Collinsville, St. Clair and Madison Counties
K Emerald Mound, Emerald Mound Road, north of Lebanon, St. Clair County. *No public access but clearly visible from the road.*
L "Floodplain mound," Illinois Route 149, west of Murphysboro, Jackson County. *No public access but clearly visible from the road.*
M Kincaid Mounds, New Cut Road, southeast of Brookport, Massac County

Prehistoric Mounds in Historic Cemeteries

N Lost Mound Cemetery, West Whitton Road, Jo Daviess County
O Oakwood Cemetery, Cass Street/Illinois Route 30, Joliet, Will County
P Woodland Cemetery, South Fifth Street, Quincy, Adams County
Q Dayton Cemetery, Eldred Road, east of Eldred, Greene County

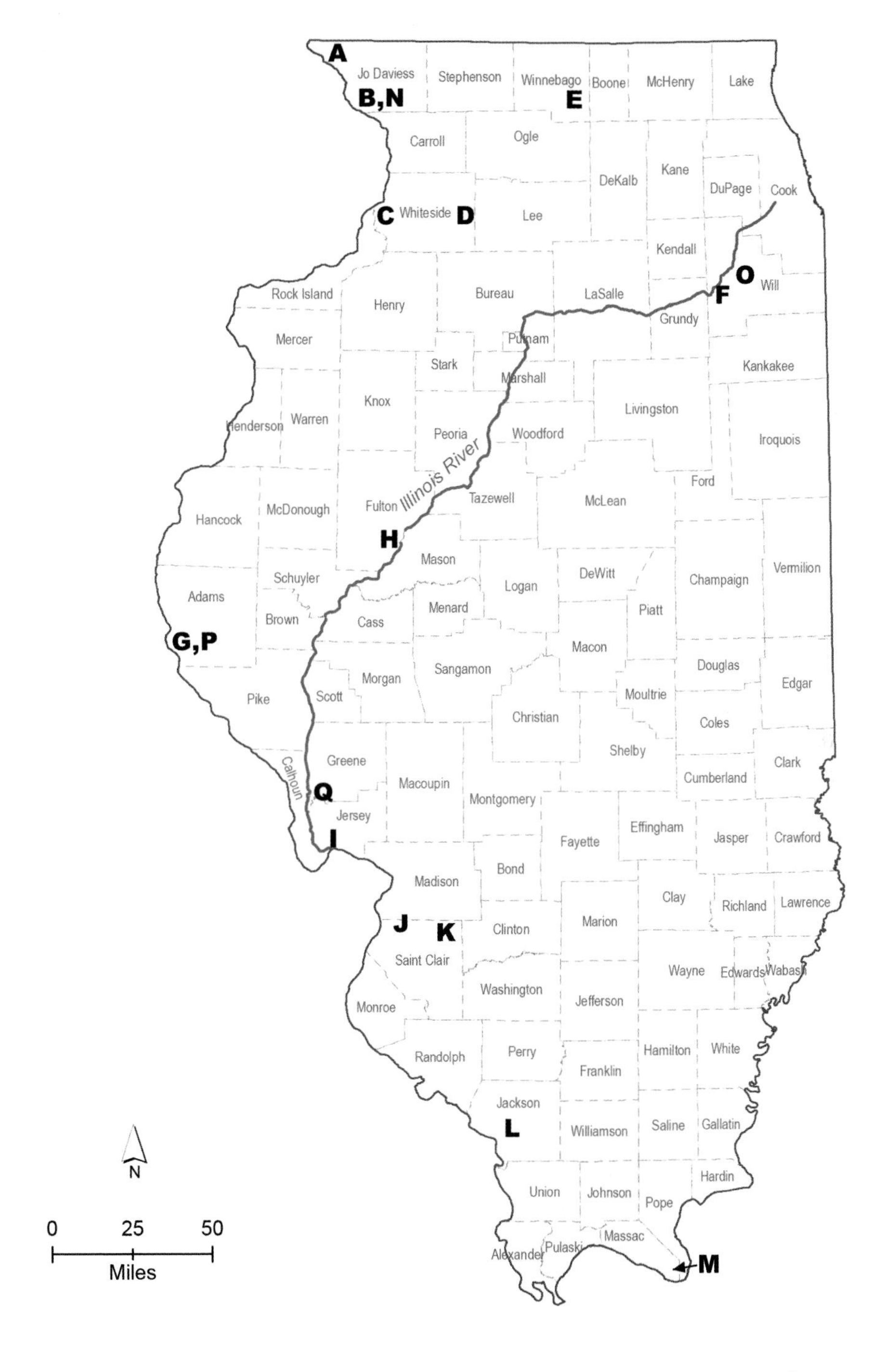

APPENDIX B
MARKER GEOLOGY

Fieldstone/Sandstone

- Composition: quartz, feldspar, mica, carbonates, and clay; conglomerate structure; soft, porous
- Color: gray, tan or brown, yellow, red, black, and white
- Texture: fine-grained to coarse-grained
- Formation: in layers as sedimentary rock
- Source: quarries in northern and southern Illinois
- Commercial uses: gravestones, tablets, building materials
- Deterioration: dissolves in acidic water, algae, lichens, plant roots, airborne grit

Rough fieldstone

Carved as grave marker

Deterioration due to lichen growth

Erosion along bedding plane

Surface erosion

Spalling surface

Slate

- Composition: clay, quartz, hematite, muscovite, pyrite; also called "black shale"; can contain fossils
- Color: light tan or shades of gray to black
- Texture: fine-grained, smooth with a platy structure
- Formation: metamorphic rock
- Source: southern Illinois, Pennsylvania, Maine, Vermont, New York, Virginia
- Commercial uses: gravestones, building, roofing, and flooring materials, tabletops, tiles, whetstones, writing slates
- Deterioration: breaks along bedding planes but resistant to water and frost damage

Carved as grave marker

Marble

- Composition: calcium or magnesium carbonate; dolomite; crystalline structure; soft, porous
- Color: white, gray, black, red, pink, brown, cream, or yellow; impurities in marble determine color
- Texture: fine-grained to coarse-grained
- Formation: metamorphic rock resulting from the recrystallization of limestone
- Source: quarries in Vermont, Georgia, Alabama, and Colorado
- Commercial uses: gravestones, building materials, statues, and sculptures
- Deterioration: dissolves in acidic water, algae, lichens, gypsum crusts, vegetation damage, airborne grit

Carved as grave marker

Carved as statue

Carved as sculpture

Weathered surface

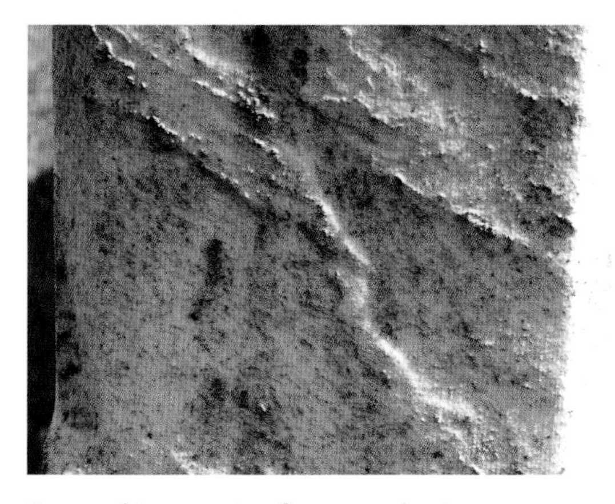

Exposed inner veins from weathering

Erosion of dove and cross

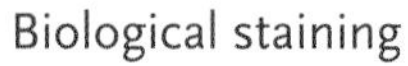

Biological staining

Vegetation damage

Limestone

- Composition: calcium carbonates with silica or clay; dolomite; contains shells of fossilized marine animals; soft, porous (softer than marble)
- Color: gray, blue-gray, white, red, brown, or green
- Texture: fine-grained to coarse-grained
- Formation: in layers as sedimentary rock
- Source: outcrops and quarries along Mississippi, Ohio, and Illinois Rivers; also found in Bedford, Indiana
- Commercial uses: gravestones, statues, sculptures, building materials, flagstone
- Deterioration: dissolves in acidic water, algae, lichens, plant roots, airborne grit

Modified into tablet marker

Detail of limestone showing fossil inclusions

Modified into statue

Modified into sculpture

Weathering of frog and tree trunk

Granite

- Composition: feldspars, quartz and mica, or hornblende; hard, dense
- Color: white, shades of gray, black, pink, red, or olive green
- Texture: fine-, medium-, or coarse-grained
- Formation: igneous rock
- Source: quarries in Minnesota, Vermont, Maine, Massachusetts, New Hampshire, Georgia, North Carolina, Texas, and California
- Commercial uses: gravestones and structural and ornamental use
- Deterioration: deteriorates in heat and pressure, biological growth

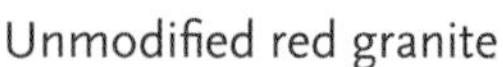
Unmodified red granite

Carved and polished red granite

Suggested Reading on Geology

Bowles, Oliver. 1934. *The Stone Industries*. New York: McGraw-Hill.

Frankie, Wayne. 2004. *Guide to Rocks and Minerals of Illinois*. Geoscience Education Series 16. Illinois State Geological Society, University of Illinois at Urbana-Champaign.

Kolata, Dennis R. 2005. *Bedrock Geology Map of Illinois*. Illinois Map 14. Illinois State Geological Survey, Urbana-Champaign.

Kolata, Dennis R., and Cheryl K. Nimz, eds. 2010. *Geology of Illinois*. University of Illinois at Urbana-Champaign, Institute of Natural Resource Sustainability, Illinois State Geological Survey.

Krey, Frank, and J. E. Lamar. 1925. *Limestone Resources of Illinois*. Department of Registration and Education, Division of the State Geological Survey, Bulletin No. 46, Urbana, Illinois.

Potter, Paul Edwin. 1962. *Late Mississippian Sandstones of Illinois*. Circular 340, Illinois State Geological Survey, Urbana.

Wiggers, Raymond. 1997. *Geology Underfoot in Illinois*. Missoula, Mo.: Mountain Press.

APPENDIX C
MARKER STYLES COMMON IN ILLINOIS

Simple

Straight head

Gothic head

Tablet head

Head with round shoulders

Head with pointed shoulders

Head with straight shoulders

Necked discoid

Obelisk

Family plot corner marker

Headstone and footstone, both with raised shoulders

Tablet-style footstone

Lawn-level

Raised top

Revolutionary War

Confederate States of America

Union Army

Composite

Head in socket

Head on base with pins

Cross-vault column

Column with urn

Late 1800s columns

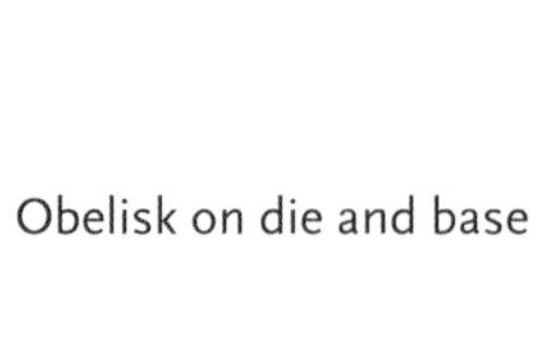

Obelisk on die and base

City vault

Family vault

Aboveground family vault

Mausoleum

Pulpit

Chair

Modern Woodmen of America

Bedstead

Scroll or “pillow”

Family plot with family marker

Box tomb of sandstone

Box tomb of sandstone

Box tomb of concrete

Box tomb of brick and mortar

NOTES

Chapter 2. Prehistoric Burial Grounds

1. Santure, Harn, and Esarey 1990.
2. Milner, Buikstra, and Wiant 2009.
3. Emerson, McElrath, and Fortier 2009.
4. Ibid.
5. Cole and Deuel 1937.
6. Pauketat 2009.

Chapter 3. Common Features of Burial Grounds

1. Stannard 1977.
2. Dethlefsen and Deetz 1966.
3. Stilgoe 1978; Stilgoe 1982.
4. McNerney and Meyer 1994; Kvale, Powell, and McNerney 2001.
5. Mueller 1976.
6. Forbes 1927; Veit and Nonestied 2008.
7. Mansberger and Stratton 2010.
8. Veit and Nonestied 2008.
9. Kvale, Powell, and McNerney 2001.
10. American Marbles 1888.
11. Gates 1934.
12. Roberts 1990; Ridlen 1996; Ridlen 1999.
13. Roberts 1990.
14. Rotundo 1995.
15. Franks 2015.
16. Clark 1987; Veit and Nonestied 2008.

17. Robinson 1890.
18. History of Government Furnished Headstones and Markers.
19. Fenza 1989.

Chapter 4. Types of Burial Grounds

1. *Webster's* 1988.
2. Oliver 1924.
3. Several publications present very good summaries on the development and organization of rural and lawn cemeteries and memorial parks. The relevant sections of this chapter are based in part on these studies, including Bender 1988; Farrell 1980; French 1975; McGuire 1988; and Sloane 1991.
4. Faust 2008.
5. Faust 2008.

Chapter 5. Grave Marker Iconography

1. Keister 2004 and Hacker 2001 are excellent sources for identifying and understanding the various iconographic images you may encounter in burial grounds. There are also numerous websites that list the images and explain their meanings; search for the phrase "cemetery motifs."
2. Forbes 1927.
3. Veit 1987.
4. Veit and Nonestied 2008.
5. Dethlefsen and Deetz 1966.
6. Deetz and Dethlefsen 1967.

SUGGESTED READINGS AND REFERENCES CITED

Suggested Readings

The number of books and articles written about burial grounds and cemeteries is vast. The suggested readings listed below focus on resources readily available in bookstores and libraries. Those who wish to pursue topics in greater depth are encouraged to consult the Association for Gravestone Studies website (https://www.gravestonestudies.org/) and in particular their publication *Markers*. The articles cover a range of topics and will provide additional references. In addition, the publications cited below contain references that can take you further into various topics.

PREHISTORIC BURIAL MOUNDS

Birmingham, Robert A., and Leslie E. Eisenberg. 2000. *Indian Mounds of Wisconsin*. Madison: University of Wisconsin Press.

Although the focus is prehistoric mounds in Wisconsin, the information is relevant to prehistoric mounds in Illinois as well.

Cole, Fay-Cooper, and Thorne Deuel. 1937. *Rediscovering Illinois: Archaeological Explorations in and around Fulton County*. Chicago: University of Chicago Press.

Describes early mound explorations in central Illinois and the development of modern archaeology in Illinois.

Emerson, Thomas E., Dale L. McElrath, and Andrew C. Fortier, eds. 2009. *Archaic Societies: Diversity and Complexity across the Midcontinent*. Albany: SUNY Press.

Contains an overview of all aspects of Archaic lifeways. The information is divided into regions to illustrate the differences and similarities among these early prehistoric people.

Perino, Gregory. 2006. *Illinois Hopewell and Late Woodland Mounds: Excavations of Gregory Perino 1950–1975*. Studies in Archaeology No. 4. Illinois Transportation Archaeology Research Program, University of Illinois at Urbana-Champaign.

Gregory Perino was an avocational archaeologist whose research has contributed invaluable knowledge about burial mounds in Illinois.

GRAVE MARKERS AND BURIAL GROUNDS

Baugher, Sherene, and Richard F. Veit. 2014. *The Archaeology of American Cemeteries and Gravemarkers.* Gainesville: University Press of Florida.

Discusses American cemeteries and burial grounds and the changes that have occurred to them in the nineteenth and twentieth centuries.

Faust, Drew Gilpin. 2008. *The Republic of Suffering: Death and the American Civil War*. New York: Vintage Press.

Tells the story of how the large number of military deaths overwhelmed the civilian population and resulted in the creation of national cemeteries.

Hucke, Matt, and Ursla Bielski. 2013. *Graveyards of Chicago: The People, History, Art, and Lore of Cook County Cemeteries*. 2nd ed. Chicago: Lake Claremont Press.

A good guide to the myriad of cemeteries found in Chicago and the surrounding Cook County communities. The reader will get a feel for their diversity of styles and history and learn where many famous people are buried.

Ridlen, Susanne E. 1999. *Tree-Stump Tombstones: A Field Guide to Rustic Funerary Art in Indiana*. Kokomo, Ind.: Old Richardville Publications.

Although the focus is Indiana, the information is also relevant to Illinois. The guide includes many illustrations of limestone markers.

Sloane, David Charles. 1991. *The Last Great Necessity: Cemeteries in American History*. Baltimore: Johns Hopkins University Press.

A detailed exploration of how American burial grounds and cemeteries changed during the nineteenth and twentieth centuries.

Veit, Richard F., and Mark Nonestied. 2008. *New Jersey Cemeteries and Tombstones*. New Brunswick, N.J.: Rivergate Books / Rutgers University Press.

An in-depth exploration of New Jersey burial grounds and cemeteries from the colonial period up to the twenty-first century. The reader will learn about changes to burial grounds outside the Midwest.

Yalom, Marilyn. 2008. *The American Resting Place: Four Hundred Years of History through Our Cemeteries and Burial Grounds*. Boston: Houghton Mifflin.

Explores the variety of burial grounds and cemeteries across the United States. Well illustrated.

GRAVE MARKER ICONOGRAPHY

Forbes, Harriette M. 1927. *Gravestones of Early New England and the Men Who Made Them, 1653–1800*. Boston: Houghton Mifflin.

An early and classic study of gravestone carvers.

Gillon, Edmund Vincent, Jr. 1966. *Early New England Gravestone Rubbings*. New York: Dover.

Provides a collection of images depicting the early art and symbolism seen in New England burial grounds. Although most are not found in Illinois, it does provide a nice comparison to earlier iconography.

Hacker, Debi. 2001. *Iconography of Death: Common Symbolism of Late Eighteenth through Early Twentieth Century Tombstones in the Southeastern United States*. Columbia, S.C.: Chicora Foundation.

Offers a variety of interpretations for gravestone images.

Keister, Douglas. 2004. *Stories in Stone: A Field Guide to Cemetery Symbolism and Iconography*. Salt Lake City: Gibbs Smith.

An excellent guide to the range of iconographic images and their meanings.

Ludwig, Allan L. 1966. *Graven Images*. Middletown, Conn.: Wesleyan University Press.

An early and still one of the best studies of New England gravestones and their carvers.

CEMETERY PRESERVATION

For those readers who are interested in historical cemetery preservation and want to experience cemeteries in more detail, the following resources offer guides to basic preservation. Please be aware that some states require permits prior to beginning a cemetery preservation project. Check with the Illinois Historic Preservation Agency, located in Springfield, to ensure that proper permits and permissions are obtained.

The Association for Gravestone Studies, www.gravestonestudies.org

Promotes the preservation of burial grounds and gravestones through their study. This national organization also has state chapters. An annual national conference highlights different regions of the United States.

Chicora Foundation, www.chicora.org

Based in South Carolina, this organization offers assistance in all aspects of cemetery preservation using a variety of disciplines—archaeology, history, landscaping, photography, and conservation.

DeBartolo Carmack, Sharon. 2002. *Your Guide to Cemetery Research*. Cincinnati: Betterway Books.

Written by a certified genealogist, the book explores a variety of topics including how to research death records, locate grave sites, and document information. It also provides an overview on burial customs and the history of cemeteries.

Hassen, Hal, and Dawn Cobb. 2009. *Illinois Historic Cemetery Preservation Handbook: A Guide to Basic Preservation*. Electronic document, http://www.illinois.gov/ihpa/Preserve/Cemetery/Documents/ILHistCemPres_9-09.pdf, accessed May 23, 2016.

Illinois Historic Preservation Agency. 2001. *Cemetery Preservation Training: Part I Basic Workshop*. Electronic document, https://www2.illinois.gov/ihpa/Preserve/Cemetery/Documents/2011CemPresTrain_P1-BWrkshp_Web.pdf.

The above two resources guide you through the steps of cemetery preservation, providing step-by-step guidance to help you plan and carry out a cemetery preservation project. An explanation of various state laws helps clarify protection and preservation of Illinois burial grounds and cemeteries.

National Center for Preservation Technology and Training, www.ncptt.nps.gov

This branch of the National Park Service provides training workshops, webinars, blogs, and national conferences to promote the conservation and preservation of cemeteries.

Strangstad, Lynette. 2013. *A Graveyard Preservation Primer*. 2nd ed. Lanham, Md.: AltaMira Press / Rowman and Littlefield.

One of the premier guides on maintaining, preserving, and repairing burial grounds. A must for anyone interested in working in a burial ground.

References Cited

American Marbles. 1888. *The Manufacture and Builder*, November: 230–231.

Bender, Thomas. 1988. The "Rural" Cemetery Movement: Urban Travail and the Appeal of Nature. In *Material Life in America 1600–1860*, edited by Robert Blair St. George, 505–518. Boston: Northeastern University Press.

Clark, Lynn. 1987. Gravestones: Reflectors of Ethnicity or Class? In *Consumer Choice in Historical Archaeology*, edited by Suzanne M. Spencer-Wood, 383–395. New York: Plenum Press.

Cole, Fay-Cooper, and Thorne Deuel. 1937. *Rediscovering Illinois: Archaeological Explorations in and around Fulton County*. Chicago: University of Chicago Press.

Deetz, James, and Edwin Dethlefsen. 1967. Death's Head, Cherub, Urn and Willow. *Natural History* 76(3), 29–37.

Dethlefsen, Edwin, and James Deetz. 1966. Death's Heads, Cherubs, and Willow Trees: Experimental Archaeology in Colonial Cemeteries. *American Antiquity* 31(40): 502–510.
Emerson, Thomas E., Dale L. McElrath, and Andrew C. Fortier, editors. 2009. *Archaic Societies: Diversity and Complexity across the Midcontinent*. Albany: SUNY Press.
Farrell, James J. 1980. *Inventing the American Way of Death*. Philadelphia: Temple University Press.
Faust, Drew Gilpin. 2008. *The Republic of Suffering: Death and the American Civil War*. New York: Vintage Press.
Fenza, Paula J. 1989. Communities of the Dead: Tombstones as a Reflection of Social Organization. *Markers* 6: 137–158.
Forbes, Harriette Merrifield. 1927. *Gravestones of Early New England and the Men Who Made Them, 1653–1800*. Boston: Houghton Mifflin.
Franks, Bob. 2015. Monuments of Iron. *Itawamba History Review*. Electronic document, http://itawambahistory.blogspot.com/search?q=monuments+of+iron, accessed October 2015.
French, Stanley. 1975. The Cemetery as Cultural Institution: The Establishment of Mount Auburn and the Rural Cemetery Movement. In *Death in America*, edited by David E. Stannard, 69–91. Philadelphia: University of Pennsylvania Press.
Gates, Paul Wallace. 1934. *The Illinois Central Railroad and the Colonization Work*. Cambridge: Harvard University Press.
Hacker, Debi. 2001. *Iconography of Death: Common Symbolism of Late Eighteenth through Early Twentieth Century Tombstones in the Southeastern United States*. Columbia, S.C.: Chicora Foundation.
History of Government Furnished Headstones and Markers. Electronic document, http://www.cem.va.gov/cem/history/hmhist.asp, accessed January 2015.
Irving, Washington. 1936. "Rip van Winkle." In *The Sketch Book*, 44. Reading, Pa.: Spencer Press.
Keister, Douglas. 2004. *Stories in Stone: A Field Guide to Cemetery Symbolism and Iconography*. New York: MFJ Books / Fine Communications.
Kvale, Erik P., Richard L. Powell, and Michael J. McNerney. 2001. *The Distribution and Carving Styles of Hindostan Whetstone Gravestones*. A final report submitted to the Indiana Historical Society.
Mansberger, Floyd, and Christopher Stratton. 2010. *Archaeological Survey Short Report: National Register of Historic Places Assessment of the Daab-Zoeller Farm Site, St. Clair County, Illinois*. Springfield, Ill.: Fever River Research. Copies available from the Illinois Historic Preservation Agency, Springfield.
McGuire, Randall H. 1988. Dialogues with the Dead: Ideology and the Cemetery. In *The Recovery of Meaning: Historical Archaeology in the Eastern United States*, edited by Mark Leone and Parker B. Potter Jr., 435–480. Washington, D.C.: Smithsonian Institution Press.
McNerney, Michael J., and Herb Meyer. 1994. *Early Pioneer Gravestones of Pope County, Illinois*. Carbondale, Ill.: American Kestrel Books.

Milner, George R., Jane E. Buikstra, and Michael D. Wiant. 2009. Archaic Burial Sites in the American Midcontinent. In *Archaic Societies: Diversity and Complexity across the Midcontinent*, edited by Thomas E. Emerson, Dale L. McElrath, and Andrew C. Fortier, 115–135. Albany: SUNY Press.

Mueller, Eileen. 1976. Two Hundred Years of Memorialization. *Monument Builders and News*, July: 6–66.

Oliver, William. 1924. *Eight Months in Illinois: With Information to Immigrants.* Originally published: Newcastle Upon Tyne, 1843. Chicago: Walter M. Hill.

Pauketat, Timothy. 2009. *Cahokia: Ancient America's Great City on the Mississippi.* New York: Viking-Penguin.

Ridlen, Susanne E. 1996. Tree-Stump Tombstones: Traditional Cultural Values and Rustic Funerary Art. *Markers* 13: 46–74.

Ridlen, Susanne E. 1999. *Tree-Stump Tombstones: A Field Guide to Rustic Funerary Art in Indiana.* Kokomo, Ind.: Old Richardville Publications.

Roberts, Warren E. 1990. Notes on the Production of Rustic Monuments in the Limestone Belt of Indiana. *Markers* 7: 173–194.

Robinson, Rowland E. 1890. In the Marble Hills (in Vermont). *Century Magazine*, September. Electronic document, *Stone Quarries and Beyond.* http://quarriesandbeyond.org/articles_and_books/in_the_marble_hills.html, accessed November 2014.

Rotundo, Barbara. 1995. Monumental Bronze: A Representative American Company. In *Cemeteries and Gravemarkers: Voices of American Culture*, edited by Richard E. Meyer, 263–291. Ann Arbor: University of Michigan Research Press.

Santure, Sharron K., Alan D. Harn, and Duane E. Esarey. 1990. *Archaeological Investigations at the Morton Village and Norris Farms 36 Cemetery.* Illinois State Museum Reports of Investigation No. 45. Springfield: Illinois State Museum.

Sloane, David Charles. 1991. *The Last Great Necessity. Cemeteries in American History.* Baltimore: John Hopkins University Press.

Stannard, David E. 1977. *The Puritan Way of Death: A Study in Religion, Culture, and Social Change.* New York: Oxford University Press.

Stilgoe, John R. 1978. Folklore and Graveyard Design. *Landscape* 22(3): 22–28.

Stilgoe, John R. 1982. *Common Landscape of America, 1580 to 1845.* New Haven, Conn.: Yale University Press.

Veit, Richard F. 1987. The New York and New Jersey Gravestone Carving Tradition. *Markers* 4: 1–54.

Veit, Richard F., and Mark Nonestied. 2008. *New Jersey Cemeteries and Tombstones: History in the Landscape.* New Brunswick, N.J.: Rivergate Books / Rutgers University Press.

Webster's New World Dictionary of American English. 1988. 3rd College Edition. New York: Simon and Schuster.

INDEX

HAL HASSEN is an archaeologist. He directed the Cultural Resource Management Program for the Illinois Department of Natural Resources from 1990 to 2015. He is coauthor, along with Dawn Cobb, of the *Illinois Historic Cemetery Preservation Handbook*.

DAWN COBB is a bio-anthropologist. She has been the director of the Cultural Resource Management Program for the Illinois Department of Natural Resources since 2016 and is a Research Associate at the Illinois State Museum.

The University of Illinois Press
is a founding member of the
Association of American University Presses.

Text designed by Jim Proefrock
Composed in 12/14 Adobe Caslon
with Optima and Scala Sans display
at the University of Illinois Press
Cover designed by Dustin J. Hubbart
Cover illustration: A family plot surrounded by
an iron fence in the Little Shepherd Cemetery,
rural Cass County. Photo by Hal Hassen.
Manufactured by Versa Press, Inc.

University of Illinois Press
1325 South Oak Street
Champaign, IL 61820-6903
www.press.uillinois.edu